ERIC BAKER

Productivity Unlocked

Making Your Unique Mind Your Greatest Asset

First published by Claims Maze Publishing Co 2025

Copyright © 2025 by Eric Baker

All rights reserved. No part of this publication may be reproduced, stored or transmitted in any form or by any means, electronic, mechanical, photocopying, recording, scanning, or otherwise without written permission from the publisher. It is illegal to copy this book, post it to a website, or distribute it by any other means without permission.

Eric Baker has no responsibility for the persistence or accuracy of URLs for external or third-party Internet Websites referred to in this publication and does not guarantee that any content on such Websites is, or will remain, accurate or appropriate.

Designations used by companies to distinguish their products are often claimed as trademarks. All brand names and product names used in this book and on its cover are trade names, service marks, trademarks and registered trademarks of their respective owners. The publishers and the book are not associated with any product or vendor mentioned in this book. None of the companies referenced within the book have endorsed the book.

First edition

ISBN: 979-8-9904647-4-2

This book was professionally typeset on Reedsy.
Find out more at reedsy.com

To my incredible kids, whose minds inspire me daily with their brilliance, creativity, and resilience—you are my greatest teachers.

To everyone who helped me grow into a more productive and compassionate version of myself—your guidance, patience, and wisdom have shaped this journey in ways I can't fully express.

To the neurodivergent community, forging paths in a world that doesn't always understand you—this book is for you.

To progress, self-discovery, and embracing the beauty in every mind.

Contents

Preface   iii
Introduction   v

I   Mindset & Motivation

1 Movement Breaks   3
2 Visual Reminders   13
3 Brain Dump Sessions   23
4 Assistive Technology   34
5 Positive Affirmations   44
6 Celebrate Small Wins   55

II   Time Management and Organization

7 Color-Coded Task Lists   69
8 Micro-Tasks   80
9 Chunk Your Time   91
10 Digital Organization Tools   102
11 Visual Timers   113
12 Mind Mapping   123

III   Routines and Accountability

13 Flexible Schedules   137
14 Body Doubling   147
15 Timed Transitions   157

16	Scheduled Check-Ins	167
17	Customize Your Routine	177
18	One Priority at a Time	188

IV Environment and Stimulus

19	Noise-Reduction Aids	201
20	Clear Physical Clutter	211
21	Sensory-Friendly Clothing	220
22	Intentional Lighting	230
23	Movement While Working	240
24	Use Labeled Storage	250

Your Mind, Your Way	259
About the Author	266

Preface

Whether you picked up this book for yourself or someone you love, you're in the right place. This is a space created for neurodivergent minds—those who think, feel, and process the world a little differently.

Maybe you're navigating ADHD, autism, dyslexia, or another unique way of experiencing life. You might be here as a partner, parent, friend, or coworker, eager to understand them more clearly and support someone you care about. Whoever you are, this book is for you.

You're not here to "fix" yourself or anyone else. Let's get that clear from the start. Neurodivergence isn't a flaw or a problem to be solved. It's a spectrum of strengths, challenges, and extraordinary ways of seeing the world.

This book isn't about forcing yourself into a mold or measuring up to someone else's definition of "productive." It's about uncovering what works for you, your rhythms, quirks, and preferences—and building a life that aligns with your unique mind.

Each chapter has been created to stand alone, like a quick, digestible guide you can dive into whenever you need. You don't have to follow a rigid order or commit to hours of reading.

Instead, use this book as a toolkit—a collection of strategies and insights you can explore at your own pace. Whether you're here for 10 minutes or an hour, read it cover to cover, or jump straight to a chapter that resonates, the choice is entirely yours.

If you're neurodivergent, you'll find tips and ideas designed to honor your strengths while addressing common challenges, all without overwhelming you with unnecessary pressure. If you love or support a neurodivergent individual, this book offers practical ways to help them thrive and insights into how their mind works.

Most importantly, this is a book about **progress, not perfection.** It's about celebrating the small wins, embracing the journey, and giving yourself (or someone you love) the space to grow in natural and sustainable ways. There's no one-size-fits-all solution, no universal "right" way to be productive. And that's the beauty of it—you get to define what works for you.

As you turn these pages, remember to **acknowledge your progress**, no matter how small it may seem. Maybe you'll discover a new tip to reduce procrastination or a hack for creating a sensory-friendly workspace. You might find comfort in the knowledge that you're not alone. Whatever you take from these chapters, know that every step forward matters.

So, welcome to this journey. Let's explore ways to honor your mind, celebrate your victories, and build a framework for a life that feels meaningful and manageable. Whether you're here to navigate your journey or walk alongside the path of someone you love, I'm so glad you've decided to join us. Let's get started!

Introduction

The aroma of freshly ground coffee beans hangs heavy in the air as Maya, Alex, and Sam huddle around a corner table at "The Daily Grind," their favorite local haunt.

Maya's brow furrows in concentration as she meticulously jots down tasks in her trusty notebook, a rainbow of color-coded entries. "Okay," she declares, "we need decorations, refreshments, and a killer playlist. Check, check, and check!"

Across the table, Alex's fingers dance across their phone screen, a symphony of taps and swipes. Virtual sticky notes, organized by color and priority, fill the screen. "Got it," Alex confirms, "I've created a shared to-do list, categorized by task and deadline."

Meanwhile, Sam's eyes sparkle with excitement, their words tumbling out in a torrent of ideas. "Guys, what if we had a photo booth with props? And a giant inflatable bouncy castle? Oh, and we could hire a mime to entertain the guests!"

Maya and Alex exchange amused glances. "Sam," Maya begins gently, "while your enthusiasm is admirable, perhaps we should focus on the essentials first?"

Alex nods in agreement. "A bouncy castle might be a bit over the top for a book club meeting, don't you think?"

Undeterred, Sam grins. "Okay, okay, maybe no bouncy castle. But the photo booth is a must! It'll be a hit!"

So, the trio continues planning, each contributing their unique skills and perspectives. Maya, the meticulous organizer, keeps everyone on track. Alex, the tech-savvy guru, ensures seamless coordination. Sam, the creative spark, injects the proceedings with a dose of infectious enthusiasm.

This is a snapshot of the human experience—a testament to the beautiful diversity of our work styles. Underneath it all is the kaleidoscope of our brains, each with its unique wiring and unique brilliance—neurodiversity.

Neurodiversity is a term that covers all kinds of brain styles. Some can focus for hours, hardly blinking until they finish a task. Others need quick bursts of activity mixed with short, playful breaks to recharge. Many people with ADHD, autism, dyslexia, or other conditions work best with unique tools and routines.

None of these brains are "wrong" or "broken." They just have different settings, like a computer with an operating system specific to that computer. Instead of seeing these differences as drawbacks, this book treats them like a pathway to discovering new ways of being productive. As we saw with those friends in the coffee shop, what works for one might not be perfect for the other.

Rethinking Traditional Methods

In many workplaces and schools, productivity often looks like a quiet desk, a to-do list with neat check boxes, and the same routine every day. But if you're someone who struggles to sit still or gets excited by new ideas faster than you can count them, these old-school methods may not fit.

You might have tried to force yourself to work in total silence, only to realize you need some background music or ambient noise to keep you from feeling restless. Or maybe you need to doodle on paper while you listen to instructions so your mind can focus.

This book offers a variety of simple, quick tactics designed for people whose brains wander—or sometimes race—at different speeds.

You'll find ideas here that range from small changes, like using sticky notes in bright colors, to bigger shifts, such as rethinking your daily schedule, so it respects your natural energy levels. You might see yourself in these pages if you have a mind that drifts off during long lectures jump from one idea to the next before you've finished what you started.

Rest assured, you're not alone. Many of these tips come from those who have found creative ways to get things done without ignoring how their brains work. This book is packed with strategies you can use and tweak to fit your needs.

A Flexible Productivity Approach

One of the main messages here is that there's no single "correct" path to productivity. If a color-coded binder excites you and gives your day structure, great! But if that same binder stresses you out and feels too rigid, it's okay to let it go. Sometimes you might hit on a strategy that feels like magic for a while, then realize it no longer works.

Maybe you tried working in 15-minute bursts and loved it, but after a few months, you need a different structure. That doesn't mean you failed. It just means your brain and situation changed, which is completely normal. When it comes to productivity, flexibility is your friend.

Of course, you'll see a lot of advice out there about getting more done in less time: set a timer, follow a strict routine, and keep your eyes on the clock. Some of those tips might be helpful for you. Others could be too harsh, especially if your motivation goes up and down like a roller coaster.

Imagine having a schedule so tight that if you're five minutes late, your whole plan falls apart. That kind of pressure can be discouraging. This book takes a different angle. Rather than forcing a one-size-fits-all system, we explore quick fixes and simple habits that you can play around with. Think of it like sampling different flavors of ice cream: you test them out and see which ones you want to take home.

You'll also see that this book is divided into clear parts: Mindset & Motivation, Time Management & Organization, Routines & Accountability, and finally Environment & Sensory.

Each section gives tips meant to work together, but you don't have to use everything. If you read about micro-tasks and realize that's exactly what you need, then focus on that. Or if you notice you're always getting distracted by the background noise in your house, jump to the section on noise-reduction aids.

The most important thing is to take these suggestions and mold them into your own life. Think of them as puzzle pieces you can arrange however you like, rather than as fixed rules you must follow.

Finding Your Superpowers

While these tips are aimed at people who identify as neurodivergent, they can help anyone who finds traditional productivity methods too narrow or boring.

Even if you don't have a formal diagnosis, you might relate to many of the concepts discussed. You might love the idea of body doubling (working near someone else) for the extra boost of motivation. Or maybe you'll find a section on assistive technology to be a game-changer if you dislike typing and prefer speech-to-text apps.

The point is to spark ideas and encourage you to try them in your day-to-day routine, seeing what makes a real difference.

If you take just one lesson from this introduction, I hope it's this: your brain isn't the problem—it's often the methods that aren't flexible enough.

Once you find a strategy that fits, work can feel smoother and more rewarding. So, grab whatever tools you like—a phone app, a pencil and paper, or a big whiteboard—and get ready to experiment. Let's shine a light on the fact that different ways of thinking can be a strength, not a weakness.

The rest of this book will walk you through small, practical steps you can try right away. You might be surprised at how a few simple changes can create a ripple effect, leading to more focus, stronger follow-through, and a new-found sense of pride.

Dive in, explore the ideas, and see how they fit your life. By the end of these chapters, you'll have a set of quick productivity hacks tailored to the way your mind works. The journey might even give you fresh insights into your brain, sparking creativity and confidence.

I

Mindset & Motivation

Think of every big journey you've heard of—it usually starts with a change in perspective. In Mindset & Motivation, we'll look at easy but powerful ways for neurodivergent minds to tap into their strengths and stay inspired.

From short movement breaks to quick brain dumps to bold visual cues, these aren't just random tricks; they're building blocks that turn everyday hurdles into steppingstones.

Laying this foundation will give you the mental boost to keep going and growing.

1

Movement Breaks

Your mind starts to drift, your shoulders slump, and you realize you've been staring at the same paragraph for ten minutes. You might think, "I have to power through." But what if taking a quick break could refresh your brain in seconds?

For many with ADHD, Autism, or the like, short bursts of movement can be the secret sauce to staying focused without feeling drained. This chapter explores why these small breaks matter, how they help you recharge, and tips on weaving them into your day.

Think of movement breaks like tiny pit stops that keep your mental engine in shape.

Why Movement Breaks Matter

Our minds thrive on a steady flow of stimulation, but sitting in one spot for too long can lead to sluggish thinking. Your body craves a reset. Standing up, stretching, or walking can jolt your energy back to life.

You might not realize it, but small changes in posture can signal the brain that it's time to wake up and refocus.

- **Improved Blood Flow:** Even a short stretch helps blood circulate, delivering oxygen to the brain.

- **Calmer Nerves:** Gentle movements can reduce stress hormones, making it easier to think clearly.

Tackling Restlessness

For those who experience restlessness, quick physical activities can channel that energy productively. Instead of fighting the urge to move, give it an outlet. A 30-second break to shake out your arms or bounce on your toes can calm the nervous system. After that, you'll often find it easier to settle back into your task.

Fighting Boredom

Sometimes, our brains simply get bored. Traditional productivity advice might say, "Stick to one place and focus." That can backfire if your mind craves variety or novelty. Movement is a simple way to add excitement to your routine, no matter how small. Each time you stand up, you shift your environment just enough to keep things interesting, giving your brain a fresh spark of attention.

Stress Reduction

Work, school, and life in general can be overwhelming. When your heart starts racing or your mind spins, a brief movement session can help. Walking to the kitchen or gently stretching in your chair allows your muscles to release tension. This mini reset can cut stress levels, so you return to your main task feeling calmer and more alert.

Quick Science Behind Short Bursts

- **Dopamine and Focus:** Physical movement can boost dopamine, a brain chemical tied to motivation and focus.
- **Mental Refresh:** Pausing to move stops your brain from getting stuck in

a loop. It's like switching channels for a moment, helping you see your work from a fresh angle.
- **Avoiding Burnout:** Long hours without breaks can cause mental fatigue. Scheduled bursts of activity let you pace yourself, preventing that "I can't do this anymore" feeling later.

It doesn't take intense exercise to reap these rewards. Simple actions—like shaking your hands—send enough signals to revitalize attention. Think of it as hitting a quick "refresh" on your mental browser.

Types of Movement Breaks

Movement breaks come in all shapes and sizes. You don't need fancy equipment or loads of time. Here are a few starter ideas.

Stand-Up Stretch

- Straighten your back, lift your arms overhead, and inhale.
- Exhale slowly, letting your shoulders drop.
- Great for anyone who finds long sessions seated uncomfortable.

Walk-Around

- Take a brisk walk down the hallway or around the block.
- Swing your arms to boost circulation.
- Perfect if you need a change of scenery.

Deskercise

- Try seated stretches if you can't leave your desk.
- Rotate your neck gently, roll your shoulders, or do a few chair twists.
- This is ideal for those with limited mobility or shared office spaces.

Mini Dance

- Put on headphones and groove to a favorite song for 30 seconds.
- Shake your arms, do a little two-step, or wiggle your hips.
- This blend of music and motion can elevate your mood quickly.

Body Scan Stretch

- Close your eyes for a moment and notice where you feel tight.
- Stretch or wiggle that area—maybe your neck, back, or ankles.
- This helps reconnect your brain with your body and reduce tension.

Setting Up a Movement Schedule

Rather than hoping you'll remember, attach a movement break to specific tasks. For example, "After finishing this email, I'll stand and stretch," or "Every time I complete two math problems, I'll do ten seconds of stretching."

By pairing movement with an activity, you make it a habit (something almost every neurodivergent mind could use) rather than an optional extra.

Time Blocking

If you use a timer or a time-blocking method, insert short activity bursts into your schedule. For example, set a 25-minute block to work, followed by stretching or walking for five minutes. Then repeat.

This approach can be helpful if you hyper-focus and lose track of time.

- **Example Pattern:** 25 minutes of work, 1 minute of movement, 4 minutes of rest. Repeat.
- **Flexibility:** If you hit a good flow, keep going. Struggling? Insert an extra movement break.

Alarms and Reminders

Forgetting is common, especially when you're deep in concentration. A simple phone alarm or computer reminder can keep you on track. Label it with a fun phrase like "Stretch Time!" so you don't ignore it. This gentle nudge ensures you don't go for hours without a break.

Movement Buddies

Sometimes a friend, coworker, or family member can help. You might send each other reminders or step outside together. If you're both working remotely, a quick text exchange— "Movement break!" —can be a fun way to stay accountable. Knowing someone else is doing it too can make it easier to follow through.

Navigating Common Challenges

"I Don't Have Enough Time"

This is a common worry. But you don't need a lengthy break, 30 seconds to a minute can do wonders. Think of these micro-breaks as investment time. By resetting your attention, you save time that might have otherwise been lost to wandering thoughts or slow progress. Start small: even one break every hour is a good start.

"I'll Lose My Concentration"

Some people fear stepping away will break a precious focus streak. But if you're truly in the zone, you can push the break a few minutes until you reach a stopping point. If you're barely hanging on to focus, a short movement break might restore the energy you need. Experiment: note how you feel before and after. You might see that a quick stretch boosts your concentration more than staying put.

"I Feel Self-Conscious"

In a shared space, you might worry people will stare if you suddenly stand up to dance. That's where more discreet stretches or a hallway walk can help. If you're in a supportive environment, invite others to join. You might be surprised how many also feel stiff or restless.

"I Overdo It and Get Distracted"

Some breaks can stretch too long—what starts as a quick walk can turn into a 30-minute internet rabbit hole. To prevent that, set a mini timer for the break itself. When the timer rings, you know it's time to refocus on the task. This balance keeps breaks truly brief.

Brain-Friendly Tips for Movement Breaks

Reward Yourself

After a day of hitting your movement goals, treat yourself to something small—like an extra 10 minutes of a favorite hobby.

Pair With Something Enjoyable

If you find stretching dull, combine it with listening to a song on your feel-good playlist. The movement becomes a pleasant break rather than a chore.

Make It Visual

Keep a sticky note on your desk saying, "Have you moved lately?" Or use a simple tally mark system to track each break. Seeing progress in real-time can be motivating to the mind.

Adapt as Needed

Find a certain stretch painful or uninteresting? Switch to something else. The goal is to find a routine that suits your body and energy.

Involve Others

Do a quick group stretch or walk with others, if possible. A shared laugh or conversation can make these breaks more enjoyable—and less likely to be skipped.

Incorporating Movement Breaks

Start Small and Build

It's tempting to go from zero to ten breaks a day. But if you're not used to it, you could forget or lose steam. Begin with one or two planned breaks and see how it feels. Once you're comfortable, add more or lengthen them slightly.

Combine with Regular Tasks

Try pairing a movement break with something you do anyway, such as getting coffee, going to the bathroom, or checking your phone messages. Each time you do that action, tag on a short movement. It becomes second nature more easily that way.

Identify High-Impact Times

Throughout the day, notice when you feel the most tired or scattered. That's when a movement break can have the biggest effect. If you always crash around 2 p.m., plan a quick stretch or walk right before that slump hits.

Keep It Fun and Flexible

No rule says you have to do the same break every time. Mix it up based on your mood or physical needs. One day might be yoga-inspired; another might be a mini dance session. Flexibility keeps your brain interested.

Benefits Beyond Work or School

Better Mood

Movement triggers the release of endorphins, often called "feel-good" chemicals. Even a brief bounce or stretch can shift your mindset, lifting your spirits and helping you approach challenges with more optimism.

Physical Health

Sitting for too long can strain your neck, back, and shoulders. Regular breaks reduce stiffness and lower the risk of longer-term aches or posture issues. Over time, these short sessions add up, contributing to overall well-being.

Social Boost

If you have friends or colleagues who also feel cooped up, you can do these breaks together—virtually or in person. Socializing for even a minute can help break the monotony. You might find that others welcome the invitation to get moving.

Sense of Control

When you take charge of your breaks, you're practicing self-care. Instead of being at the mercy of restlessness or boredom, you decide when and how you'll move. This can build confidence and remind you that you have agency in your daily routine.

Overcoming Guilt

Some people worry that any pause is "wasted time." But productivity isn't just about hours logged, it's about work quality.

If a 30-second stretch helps you focus more deeply, it's not a waste, it's a tool. By allowing yourself these mini breaks you're preventing burnout, mistakes, and the sluggishness that creeps in after too much sitting.

Guilt can be a tough habit to break, so try re-framing your mindset: *these movement intervals are investments, not indulgences.*

Putting It All Together

Movement breaks might seem trivial, but they can make a real difference in daily life—especially for neurodivergent minds that juggle restlessness, focus shifts, or sensory overload.

Here's a quick recap to keep in mind:

- **Small Moves, Big Impact:** Even 15-30 seconds of stretching can recharge your brain.
- **Adapt to Your Style:** Whether you prefer low-key chair stretches or a mini dance, find what suits your energy level.
- **Set Reminders:** Alarms, sticky notes, or habit trackers can nudge you when you forget.
- **Pair With Tasks or Times:** Link movement to routine tasks or known slump periods for best results.
- **Respect Your Body:** Feel pain or discomfort? Opt for gentle moves. If you have energy to burn, go for a faster pace.
- **Celebrate Wins:** When you remember to move, you reinforce a healthy habit. Acknowledge your Progress.

Think of these breaks like pressing "refresh" on a web page. When your screen starts to freeze, you don't sit and stare; you do something to reboot.

The same goes for your focus and energy levels. Standing up, stretching, and walking around are all ways to hit that mental refresh button.

Once you start using movement breaks consistently, you'll likely see improvements in clarity, mood, and overall motivation.

You might also notice less tension in your neck and shoulders and a more relaxed approach to stressful tasks. And if you ever slip up and forget, don't worry—just get back on track when you remember.

Over time, these small bursts of activity can become second nature, keeping your mind sharper and your energy steadier throughout the day.

Movement breaks are easy, free, and adaptable. They fit nearly any lifestyle and energy level, making them one of the simplest productivity hacks. Give them a try and see how small actions can yield big results in how you work, learn, and live.

2

Visual Reminders

Stop for a moment and think of the objects that catch your eye every day. A bright poster on the wall, a colorful mug on your desk, or a bold sign at a store.

These images grab our attention because our brains are naturally drawn to vivid or eye-catching visuals. This is especially true for neurodivergent minds that crave clear cues or quick reminders to stay on track.

Visual reminders can help keep important tasks at the forefront, so you don't lose track or feel overwhelmed. In this chapter, we'll explore using sticky notes, bold visuals, and strategic placement to create an environment that works with, rather than against, a wandering or hyperactive mind.

Why Visual Reminders Matter

Many people rely on apps, calendars, and lists to manage tasks. While those tools can be helpful, they often stay hidden behind a phone screen or tucked inside a planner. It makes it easier for them to be forgotten altogether.

Visual reminders are different. They live in your field of vision, acting like friendly signposts that say, "Hey, don't forget me." For example, a sticky note on your bathroom mirror might remind you to take vitamins or respond to an important email before you leave the house.

The "spicy" neurodivergent minds sometimes struggle with working memory or experience frequent mental detours. Visual aids can fill that gap by putting critical information right where your eyes land.

The mind processes images quickly, which can be advantageous if you often feel pulled in multiple directions. Instead of digging through a mental or digital list to recall what's next, you see it immediately.

It's less about brute force memory and more about adapting your space to guide you. Visual reminders also tap deeper into your mind: the love for color, patterns, and fun.

When you pair a task with a bright note or striking graphic, you're injecting energy into your day. That spark can be just enough to push you toward action.

This approach can work well whether your schedule is jam-packed or loosely structured. In either case, bright visuals offer little nudges that can keep you from drifting off course.

The Brain's Attraction to Color and Contrast

Think of the last time you saw a neon sign on a busy street. Even if you weren't interested in the sign's message, you probably glanced at it because it was hard to ignore. Our brains are wired to notice contrast and vivid hues. For neurodivergent individuals who might already scan their surroundings in unique ways, color-based cues can be a fantastic tool.

- **Color as a Category:** Try to use color-coding to separate tasks by urgency or category. Bright yellow for items that need attention, green for creative projects, or pink for personal chores. At a glance, you see which tasks belong where.
- **Emotional Boost:** Certain colors can lift your mood. A pleasant blue or sunny orange might bring calm or spark energy.
- **Immediate Recognition:** If you always use lime green sticky notes for tasks that need attention, your brain will learn to zero in on them.

By harnessing color and contrast, you craft an environment that speaks directly to your visual senses. Using color helps keep important tasks from blending into the background.

Just make sure you pick colors that don't overload your senses. If loud reds or bright yellows feel jarring, opt for softer but distinct shades.

You want something that catches your eye without overwhelming it.

Sticky Notes: Small but Mighty

There's a reason sticky notes are a classic tool for reminders. They're easy to place, easy to remove, and come in a rainbow of colors. You can jot down a single word or a short sentence, stick it to a visible surface, and have a quick heads-up whenever you walk by.

For neurodivergent minds that often need gentle nudges, sticky notes can be powerful allies.

Getting the Most Out of Sticky Notes

Keep It Short

Write just a few words—something like "Call Dad," "Upload Report," or "Take Vitamins." The simpler the note, the easier it is to process at a glance.

Rotate Them Regularly

The brain adapts to seeing the same thing repeatedly, eventually treating it as background noise.

If you keep a note in the same spot for too long, you might stop noticing it. Refresh or move them every few days, even if it's just an inch or two away.

Group Similar Tasks

If you have three sticky notes for errands, cluster them together in one area. That way, you see them as a mini set rather than scattered bits that your eyes might skip over.

Use Different Shapes

If regular squares start blending in, try heart-shaped or arrow-shaped notes. Novelty can keep your interest alive. Sticky notes work because they're flexible, fun, and easily re-positioned.

They can turn any surface (i.e. a mirror, laptop lid, or door) into a quick alert system for your day-to-day tasks.

Bold Visuals

While sticky notes are a solid option, sometimes you need bigger or bolder visuals to catch your eye. This can be especially true if you find yourself craving extra mental stimulation or if smaller reminders quickly become "visual clutter."

Whiteboards or Chalkboards

- **Flexible Canvas:** Jot down tasks, appointments, or even doodles. Erase and rewrite as needed.
- **Colorful Markers:** Use different colors for different task types—red for work deadlines, blue for personal to-dos, and green for fun projects.
- **Position Matters:** Place the board where your gaze naturally falls. This could be near your desk, in the kitchen, or close to the entryway.

Poster-Style Reminders

- **Graphic Elements:** Print a phrase like "Remember to Breathe!" in a large, eye-catching font and hang it up.
- **Inspirational Images:** Combine a task reminder with an uplifting photo or illustration; a reminder to drink water beside a photo of a waterfall or ocean scene.

Collage Boards or Vision Boards

- **Goal-Oriented:** If you're working toward a bigger goal—writing a book, planning a trip, or launching a small business—a collage board can keep that vision front and center.
- **Frequent Updates:** Add or remove images as your goals shift, so it remains fresh and engaging.

Colorful Calendars

- **Wall Calendars:** Hang a large monthly calendar in a common space. Use vibrant stickers or markers to note important dates.
- **Magnetic Calendars:** If you have a metal surface like a fridge, a magnetic version can be handy and easy to reconfigure. Bold visuals cater to people who prefer something more substantial than a small note. If you're someone who likes a constant, bigger-picture view, these methods can keep you inspired and on track.

Placing Reminders in the Right Spots

Even the most stunning reminder won't do you any good if it's hidden in a corner you rarely notice. The art of placement is key. Think about your daily routine: where do your eyes naturally go? Where do you tend to pause for a moment?

- **Entryway:** A note on the inside of your front door can remind you to grab your keys, feed the cat, or return library books.
- **Bathroom Mirror:** Perfect spot for quick daily tasks—taking meds, flossing, or listening to that new audio book you keep forgetting about.
- **Above Your Desk:** A prime location if you spend a lot of time working or studying. Keep essential tasks at eye level so you're reminded of them regularly.
- **Fridge or Kitchen Counter:** Great for grocery lists, meal prep reminders, or healthy eating prompts.

Avoid Overloading a Single Space

It's easy to get carried away and plaster an entire door or wall with notes. That can backfire because it might turn into a blur of colors your brain tunes out. Instead, spread out your reminders based on where the task is most relevant. If your job is to water the plants, put a note near where you keep the watering can.

Avoiding Visual Clutter

Visual reminders are helpful only if they remain clear and organized. When you pile too many things into one area, the messages lose their power. Clutter can be frustrating for many who may already feel overloaded by sensory input.

Limit the Quantity

Ask yourself which tasks are truly high priority. Focus your visual reminders on those. You don't need a sticky note for every single chore, or you risk burying the big stuff.

Use Clear Labels

If you're posting notes or signs, keep the wording concise. "Clean Desk," "Pay Rent," or "Meeting at 3 PM" are easy to digest. Long paragraphs can become too heavy.

Regular Refresh

Once you've completed a task, remove the note right away. If you leave it in place, your space might fill up with old reminders that no longer matter. Maintaining a balance is vital. You want enough reminders to keep you on top of things but not so many that your environment feels chaotic.

Tools and Materials to Explore

Whether you prefer small sticky notes or giant posters, there are plenty of options to consider. Here's a quick rundown of items that can help you create an effective reminder system:

- **Sticky Notes:** Affordable and easy to reposition.
- **Index Cards:** Slightly sturdier than sticky notes and good for more detailed reminders or short checklists.
- **Whiteboards:** Reusable surfaces ideal for quickly updating tasks.
- **Magnetic Boards:** Useful if you like to move small magnets or shape magnets for tasks.
- **Colored Tape:** Mark off sections of a wall or desk to create "zones" for different types of tasks.
- **Bulletin/Cork Boards:** Pin up notes, photos, or small objects that represent tasks.
- **Washable Window Markers:** Write your reminders on glass surfaces, such as windows or mirrors, then wipe them clean when you're done.

Choosing the right tools often depends on your personal preference. Some like the tactile feel of paper, while others prefer boards that can be easily erased. If something isn't working for you, switch it up. The goal is to find what feels most natural and supportive.

Digital Visuals

Physical reminders aren't the only way to keep tasks in front of you. If you're someone who spends a lot of time on digital devices, electronic visuals might work better.

- **Computer Wallpaper:** Design a simple wallpaper with key reminders like one to help you remember movement breaks.
- **Virtual Sticky Notes:** Many operating systems have built-in sticky note apps you can pin to your desktop.
- **Browser Extensions:** Tools like Momentum or other new tab extensions can display goals or a to-do list each time you open a new browser tab.
- **Widget Reminders:** On phones or tablets, add reminder widgets to your home screen.
- **Digital Kanban Boards:** Apps like Trello let you see tasks in columns, which provide a visual layout that's easy to grasp at a glance.

Digital options can help people who are always on a computer or phone. Just be sure they don't get buried under other windows or apps. Think about setting them to "always on top," or placing them in a location you'll see first.

Making It a Habit

One of the biggest challenges is not setting up the reminders, but remembering to keep them updated. Visual reminders are only effective if they reflect your current priorities. Here are some tips to develop a solid habit:

- **Set a Weekly "Refresh" Time:** Pick a day—maybe Sunday morning—when you'll spend 10 minutes reviewing and updating all your notes or

boards. Clear out anything that's done. Add upcoming tasks to keep your system relevant.
- **Keep It Manageable:** Avoid turning your reminder system into another lengthy to-do. Make it quick and simple. The idea is to stay agile, not to spend half an hour reorganizing notes each day.
- **Celebrate Small Progress:** When you see a note that says, "Complete Presentation," and you get it done, let yourself feel good about removing that note or marking it as finished. A small sense of accomplishment can fuel motivation to keep using the system.

Troubleshooting Common Issues

Visual Overload

If your walls look like a collage of sticky papers, it might be time to scale back. Choose a few top tasks to feature and store the rest in a more private list.

Forgetting to Look

Sometimes we get so used to seeing reminders that we overlook them. Moving items or switching up colors can rekindle your attention.

Too Many Platforms

If you're using physical sticky notes, three apps, a whiteboard, plus a phone calendar, you might get confused about which system to trust. Try consolidating into one main system with smaller supporting elements.

Clashing with Others

If you share your space with roommates or family, bright notes everywhere might annoy them. Consider setting up a personal station—a desk corner or bulletin board—so your visuals don't sprawl too much into shared spaces.

Summing It All Up

Visual reminders are like little spotlights directing your attention to what matters most. For neurodivergent minds—prone to distractions or unique thought patterns—these spotlights can be incredibly powerful. By using sticky notes, color-coding, or larger visuals like whiteboards and posters, you create a system that keeps key tasks in plain sight.

The trick is to find a balance: **enough reminders to guide you without burying you in visual noise.** When placed in the right spots, these notes or signs can catch your eye at precisely the moment you need them—reminding you of an upcoming deadline, an important errand, or a positive affirmation about your goals.

With regular updates, clear zones for different types of tasks, and a consistent plan for removing old reminders, you can maintain an environment that feels supportive rather than cluttered. It's easy to underestimate the power of simple visuals, yet they've been a staple for students, professionals, and busy families for decades because they work. Adding your own twist—like minimalistic color schemes, small rewards, or using icons you love—turns this approach into a personal productivity tool that aligns with how your mind operates.

So go ahead, grab some sticky notes, place them where you're most likely to see them and let them guide you through the day's tasks. Pay attention to what feels good and what feels cluttered, then adjust as you go. Before long, you might find that what started as a few bright pieces of paper has transformed your space into a helpful, motivating environment.

That's the power of visual reminders—keeping your tasks visible, your goals close at hand, and your mind free to explore, create, and **get things done.**

3

Brain Dump Sessions

It might help you to imagine your mind as a busy city. There are streets filled with everyday tasks, side alleys loaded with personal worries, and towering skyscrapers representing your biggest hopes and dreams.

Sometimes, the traffic of thoughts in this "city" can get jammed. You want to focus on a specific goal, but random ideas zoom around, making it tough to concentrate. Brain dump sessions offer a simple way to clear that mental traffic.

By writing everything down—big or small—you free space in your mind, allowing you to plan and act with clarity. This chapter shows why these sessions matter and how to turn a jumble of ideas into a list that helps you move forward.

Why Brain Dumps Are So Powerful

Quieting the Mental Chatter

Many of us carry thoughts around like a giant backpack that gets heavier as the day goes on. You might worry about returning a library book, cooking dinner, finishing a work project, and replying to a friend's text. Each item takes up space, even if it's small.

Doing a brain dump means you lay those worries on paper instead of letting them bounce around in your head. It's a release valve, letting out the pressure that builds when your brain juggles too many tasks. When your head feels overcrowded, it's easy to forget important details or lose track of priorities.

A quick brain dump session helps you see what's actually on your mind. Instead of wrestling with fleeting thoughts, you have them listed. It's a bit like de-cluttering in a messy room. Once everything is out in the open, you can decide what needs your attention and what can wait.

Great for Neurodivergent Minds

For many with neurodivergent minds, concentration can be a winding road rather than a straight path. Thoughts can appear suddenly, demand attention, and vanish just as quickly. Brain dump sessions can bring order to the chaos.

In a short burst of writing, you let your mind wander across the page instead of your daily life. The ideas that might have tormented you at night or distracted you during work are now in a safe spot.

People often overlook how stressful it can be to carry loose ends. You might recall a random detail at 2 a.m. or keep replaying an errand in your mind until you're afraid you'll forget it.

A brain dump is a security blanket for your thoughts—it's all there on paper, so you won't lose anything. This safety net can help reduce feelings of anxiety or restlessness, since you know those ideas aren't going anywhere.

How to Perform a Brain Dump

Creating the Right Space

Set aside a few minutes in a comfortable spot. Some people like doing this early in the morning, while others prefer late at night to clear their thoughts before sleeping. Pick a notebook or loose sheets of paper—anything that feels inviting. If you prefer typing, open a blank document on your computer or a note on your phone. The method you choose should feel natural.

The goal is to make it easy to capture your thoughts without overthinking the process. It can help to avoid distractions for this short time. Turn off your TV, silence notifications, or put on calming music if that helps. The idea is to let your brain flow freely. If you're in a noisy environment and can't change that, consider wearing noise-canceling headphones or listening to gentle background sounds. Whatever reduces mental clutter so you can focus on unloading your thoughts.

Let Your Thoughts Pour Out

Once you're ready, start writing everything that comes to mind. Don't worry about grammar, spelling, or structure. If you think about needing groceries, write it down. If you remember a conversation you need to finish, jot that down too. Random worries, daydreams, and tasks all belong here. This isn't a formal essay or your to-do list; it's a safe dumping ground for whatever is clogging your mental channels. You might find yourself writing sentences like:

- "Pick up cat food"
- "Call Aunt Maria about the birthday party"
- "Research new job ideas"
- "Still upset about that argument last week"

Let it flow until you feel your mind start to calm. Some days it might take five minutes, other times you might fill several pages. There's no wrong or right amount.

Brain Dump Methods to Explore

Not everyone does a brain dump in the same way. Here are a few popular approaches, each with a twist that might suit different styles or preferences.

Free-Flow Paragraph

- Write in long-form paragraphs.
- Let your mind wander.
- Good for those who think in a stream-of-consciousness style.

Bullet-Point Blitz

- List everything in short bullet points.
- Quick and efficient.
- Ideal for minds that hop from one thought to the next rapidly.

Mind Map

- Write your central thought in the middle of a page.
- Branch out with lines for sub-thoughts.
- Great for visual thinkers who like to see connections.

Themed Brain Dumps

- Divide your page into sections: Work, Home, Personal, Social, etc.
- Empty your thoughts into each box.
- Helps if you like categorizing as you go.

Voice Notes

- Use a voice recording app if writing feels slow.
- Talk about anything on your mind.
- Later, you can transcribe or listen back to pick out key points.

Random Thoughts into Action Items

Identify the Clusters

After your brain dump, you might have pages of random ideas. First, skim through what you wrote and look for related themes. Maybe you have multiple points about errands or repeated worries about an upcoming meeting. Draw a highlight or circle items that connect. This helps you see patterns and figure out which areas need attention.

For example: "Buy cat food," "Refill prescription," and "Pick up dry cleaning" could all form an "errands" category.

Decide on the Next Steps

Each cluster might contain tasks you can act on right away. Others might be more long-term or emotional. Sort them into these types:

1. **Immediate Tasks:** Things you can tackle today or tomorrow—like paying a bill or scheduling an appointment.
2. **Ongoing Projects:** Bigger goals that need chunking into micro-steps—like "Write a chapter of my book" or "Plan a vacation."
3. **Ideas to Explore Later:** Some thoughts might not need action now, but you don't want to forget them. Store them in a separate note or file labeled "future ideas."
4. **Emotional or Reflective Thoughts:** Worries or deeper concerns may need reflection, a chat with a friend, or professional help. Keep them in a "personal reflections" category for now.

Assign Priorities

Not every item on your list has the same urgency. Star or highlight anything that must be done soon. If you have a digital task manager, transfer high-priority tasks into it. If you prefer paper planners, write them down in your daily to-do list. This part transforms random ideas into an organized plan. Instead of feeling scattered, you now know what to handle first and what can wait.

Why This Matters

Preventing Overload

For many neurodivergent people, small tasks can pile up quickly in the mind, creating an overwhelming sense of confusion. Brain dumps act like a net for all that mental clutter, providing a safe spot for it to land. Once it's written down, you free your brain to focus on what's truly in front of you. This approach can reduce moments of panic when you suddenly realize you forgot an important detail.

Building Confidence

Checking off items from your brain dump can be a huge boost. Instead of having a vague sense of "I'm behind on everything," you see the real picture. Even if you have 20 items, at least they're concrete. You can tackle them one by one. Each time you cross something out, you get a small win that fuels motivation. Over time, you gain confidence in your ability to handle day-to-day tasks without losing track.

Encouraging Reflection

Neurodivergent minds sometimes jump between thoughts quickly, making it hard to process emotions or bigger life questions. Brain dump sessions can slow you down enough to notice patterns in your worries or hopes. Maybe you see that you've written "Find a new hobby" multiple times. That might be a clue that you're craving a creative outlet. Spotting these hints can guide you toward activities or changes that improve your well-being.

Avoiding the Traps

Overthinking the Process

Some folks worry they're "doing it wrong." Remember, there's no perfect method for a brain dump. The core idea is to capture thoughts without judgment. Don't get hung up on neatness. Stick to whatever style flows.

Forgetting to Review

A brain dump only helps if you look back at it. Schedule a quick review—maybe once a day or once a week. This ensures that important tasks don't remain buried.

Making It Too Complicated

If you end up with color-coded spreadsheets or a massive binder, you might lose the simple beauty of the process. Keep it straightforward. If fancy systems help you, that's great, but it's not a requirement.

Failing to Take Action

After brain dumping, you might feel relieved but never turn items into doable tasks. Remember to sort your notes, pick your priorities, and move them into whatever system you use for daily planning.

Slipping Back into Mental Storage Mode

It's common to start strong with brain dumps but later revert to carrying everything in your head again. Regular check-ins—maybe a weekly "brain dump session" on Sundays—help keep the habit alive.

Part of Your Routine

Scheduled Sessions

Some people do a brain dump first thing in the morning as a way to clear out leftover thoughts from the night. Others prefer bedtime to free their mind to get restful sleep. Or you could aim for two or three short sessions throughout the day—especially if you sense mental overload creeping in. Consistency is key. Once you find a time that works, stick with it so it becomes second nature.

Pair It With Another Habit

One trick is to link a brain dump to a habit you already do. For instance, whenever you finish lunch, you could set aside five minutes to jot down any swirling thoughts. Or right after you brush your teeth at night, do a quick recap of the day's concerns and to-dos. Habit pairing makes it easier to remember that it's time to unload your mind.

Use Tools You Love

Make the session enjoyable by using tools that appeal to your senses. If you adore the feel of pen on paper, invest in a nice notebook or fun-colored pens. If technology is your comfort zone, find a minimalistic app with a clean interface. Some apps offer voice-to-text options, letting you speak your thoughts instead of typing. If you look forward to the process, you're more likely to keep it up.

Extra Tips and Tricks

Keep It Fun

Nobody said this has to be boring. Stickers, doodles, and colored highlights can add a creative flair. If you like drawing, include small sketches. Visual elements can help certain folks process thoughts more effectively.

Accept the Mess

Sometimes your notes will appear sloppy or chaotic. That's fine. Brain dumps are about expression, not perfection. Focus on capturing ideas quickly. You can tidy up later if it's needed.

Consider a "Midday Reset"

If you're someone who experiences an afternoon energy slump, a quick brain dump around lunchtime might clear your head for the rest of the day. You release distractions before diving into the next block of tasks.

Use Timers

Set a timer for five or ten minutes. Knowing you have a set window can push you to empty your mind fast, without pausing to judge or censor your thoughts. When the timer rings, you have a fuller picture of what's been swirling in your head.

Combine with Gratitude or Affirmations

After listing your worries and tasks, jot down one or two things you're thankful for or proud of. This can balance out the sometimes heavy load of to-dos and concerns. You end the session on a positive note.

Brain Dump Questions

- **How often should I do a brain dump?** It varies. Some people find once a week enough, others need daily sessions, and some do multiple quick dumps throughout the day. Experiment and see what fits your lifestyle.
- **What if I don't have much to write?** That's okay. Some days your mind might not be overflowing. Write whatever comes—even if it's just "I'm worried I'll forget something." The act of checking in with yourself is still valuable.
- **Should I go digital or stick to paper?** Use whatever feels comfortable. Paper can be more tactile and grounding, while digital notes are easy to search and organize. You might even switch between both as needed.
- **Do I need a fancy planner or notebook?** No. A simple piece of printer paper works fine. If a nice planner motivates you, go for it, but it's not mandatory. The key is to capture your thoughts in a way that feels natural.
- **How do I know if I'm making progress?** Notice if you feel calmer or more organized after your sessions. Over time, you might find you forget fewer tasks or feel less anxious. That's a good sign you're on the right track.

The Lasting Value of Brain Dumps

Brain dump sessions aren't just about offloading random ideas—they're about creating mental space. Once that space opens up, you can see where your focus should be. For neurodivergent minds, or anyone juggling a busy life, this practice can be a powerful tool in managing day-to-day responsibilities. You no longer rely solely on memory, which can falter under stress or distraction. Instead, you have a clear snapshot of what's rattling around in your head.

By reviewing your brain dumps, grouping related items, and turning them into actionable tasks, you lay the groundwork for real productivity. You move from feeling scattered to feeling purposeful. That sense of control can bring relief, confidence, and better balance. Even better, you start to notice patterns—recurring worries, repeated goals, or neglected passions. Each session becomes a window into your inner world.

Brain dumps can be as simple or as detailed as you want. Some prefer short bullet lists, while others like in-depth journaling. The beauty is that it's adaptable. No matter how messy or fast your thoughts come, they'll find a place on paper (or a screen) during these sessions. Over time, you might find this habit becomes second nature. You realize you can face challenges with a clearer mind because you aren't dragging around a cluttered mental load.

In the end, brain dump sessions are about more than productivity. They're about well-being. They create breathing room for your thoughts, giving you a chance to see them clearly and decide what to do next. That clarity helps you handle life's demands with a calmer, more focused mindset. Remember we are after **progress, not perfection.**

It all starts with one simple step: grab a pen or open a blank file, and let those thoughts flow.

#　4

Assistive Technology

Picture walking into a library filled with endless books, each holding a wealth of information. Now imagine if you couldn't easily turn those pages or had difficulty reading the text. That's where assistive technology steps in, acting like a personal helper who can flip the pages or even read them to you.

For many with neurodivergent traits, tools like text-to-speech or speech-to-text can be life-changing. They ease the struggles that arise from reading and writing challenges, helping you unlock your full potential. In this chapter, we'll explore common assistive tech options and offer tips on how to weave them smoothly into daily life.

What Is Assistive Technology?

Assistive technology is any tool, software, or device that helps you do something more easily, especially if you face challenges in certain tasks. When people hear this term, they might picture advanced gadgets or pricey devices. The truth is, that a lot of helpful tech is available for free or at a small cost. At its core, assistive technology aims to make life simpler and more accessible—no fancy equipment required.

Why It Matters for Neurodivergent Minds

Reading, writing, or even focusing on tasks can feel like an uphill climb for people with ADHD, dyslexia, autism, or related conditions. Rather than fighting these struggles alone, assistive tech steps in like a friendly hand. If you find reading blocks of text draining, text-to-speech can narrate the words aloud. If writing your thoughts on paper is time-consuming, speech-to-text can capture them instantly as you speak. These tools can be especially helpful in school, at work, or home when you want to communicate or learn without being slowed down by format or focus issues.

The Power of Listening

Text-to-Speech

Text-to-speech (TTS) converts written text into spoken words. You can highlight a passage on your screen, press a button, and hear it read in a digital voice. Some systems let you pick different voices or adjust speed and pitch. That means you can speed through a long article if you're in a hurry or slow it down for better clarity.

Who Benefits

- **Dyslexia or Reading Challenges:** Individuals who mix up letters or find words dancing on the page can relax and absorb information by listening.
- **ADHD or Limited Focus:** If you lose focus reading from a screen, hearing the text might keep your mind engaged. You can even do light tasks—like folding laundry—while listening.
- **Visual Overload:** Some people find large blocks of text overwhelming. Having it spoken aloud can reduce eye strain and mental fatigue.

Tips for Daily Use

- **Browser Extensions:** Several free extensions read web articles aloud. Look for ones that let you highlight only the parts you need.
- **Smartphones and Tablets:** Most modern devices include a "Speak Screen" or "Text-to-Speech" feature in the accessibility settings. Turn it on and experiment with the settings.
- **E-Readers:** Apps like Kindle or other e-book platforms often have a built-in TTS option. Use it for textbooks, novels, or even personal documents.

Talking Your Way to Clarity

Speech-to-Text

Speech-to-text (STT), also called voice recognition, transcribes your spoken words into digital text. You talk, and the software types it out. Many phones, tablets, and computers come with voice dictation built in. There are also specialized apps that let you speak notes or longer documents, and then edit them afterward.

Who Could Use STT

- **Difficulty Writing or Typing:** This might be due to dysgraphia, motor skill challenges, or simply the frustration of capturing thoughts quickly.
- **Busy Thinkers:** If your mind races with ideas, speaking them out loud can keep pace better than typing.
- **People on the Go:** You can dictate notes while walking or doing errands, turning downtime into productive brainstorming.

Daily STT Tips

- **Clear Speech:** Speak at a steady pace, enunciate words, and include phrases like "comma," "period," or "new line" for punctuation.
- **Double-Check for Errors:** Voice recognition is good but not perfect. Look for odd word choices or missed punctuation. A quick edit can polish your text.
- **Integrate with Apps:** Many note-taking apps have a built-in microphone icon. Tap it to start dictating, then review the text later.

Reading Tools and Extensions

Special Fonts and Backgrounds

Some with dyslexia, or other reading difficulties, benefit from specialized fonts (like OpenDyslexic or Lexend-the font I used for this text) designed to reduce letter confusion. Changing the page background color can also help the eyes track lines more smoothly. Light yellow or pastel backgrounds often reduce glare, making text easier to follow.

Summarizers and Simplifiers

Have you ever faced a dense document and wished it could be explained in simpler words? Certain browser extensions or apps can summarize articles, stripping them down to main points. Others rephrase text at a lower reading level. These tools can be lifesavers if you find heavy text challenging or time-consuming.

Annotation and Highlighting

For many neurodivergent learners, active reading is key. You might need to highlight phrases or jot notes in the margin to stay focused. Digital annotation tools allow you to do this on a screen—using colors, underlining, or sticky note features. This method keeps your mind engaged and helps recall key ideas later.

Practical Suggestions

- **Browser Plugins:** Tools like "Mercury Reader" (removes clutter) or "Read Aloud" can simplify and speak text.
- **E-Reader Features:** Kindle and other apps let you highlight words, see definitions, or add notes.
- **Mind Mapping Software:** After reading a page, use a mind map to capture key themes in a visual layout.

Writing Tools and Editors

Spell Checkers and Grammar Helpers

Even experienced writers slip up, but for those who have dyslexia, ADHD, or other language-based differences, small errors can pile up quickly. Tools like Grammarly, ProWritingAid, or built-in spell checkers offer real-time feedback. They often give suggestions for grammar, word choice, and clarity. This immediate guidance can sharpen your writing without the frustration of scanning line by line on your own.

Word Prediction Software

Some programs predict the word you're typing before you finish, which helps if you often struggle with spelling or pick the wrong term. The software learns from your writing style and suggests likely choices. This speeds up typing and cuts down on errors.

Formatting Aids

Many people have trouble structuring essays or documents. Apps and add-ons can guide you through building an outline, choosing section headings, or even generating a table of contents. This can be especially helpful if organizing your thoughts feels like herding cats.

Making It Work for You

- **Trial Different Tools:** Most writing apps offer a free version or trial period. Experiment to see which interface suits you best.
- **Don't Over-Rely on Corrections:** Even the best tech can guess wrong. Always do a final check to ensure the tool isn't inserting odd words.
- **Set Preferences:** If you know you often misuse homophones (like "their" vs. "there"), tell the software to watch for those specifically.

Part of Your Daily Routine

Start with One or Two Tools

It's tempting to install a bunch of apps and extensions all at once. That can feel overwhelming fast. Pick one or two that address your biggest pain points. Maybe you struggle most with reading long documents, so you try text-to-speech. Or perhaps organizing tasks is your main hurdle, so you begin with a calendar tool.

Practice and Adjust

Like learning a musical instrument, mastering assistive tech takes practice. For instance, speech-to-text might misinterpret certain words until you learn to speak more clearly or adjust your microphone settings. Give yourself time to experiment, make mistakes, and refine your technique.

Build a Habit Loop

Pair the use of an assistive tool with a daily activity. For example, if you want to use text-to-speech for reading news articles, do it every morning when you open your laptop. If you plan to track your tasks in Trello, update your board right after dinner. Turning tool usage into a habit means you'll continue benefiting rather than forgetting about it after a week.

Share Your Experience

If you have friends, classmates, or colleagues also navigating reading or writing challenges, swap tips. They might suggest a browser extension you haven't tried, or you could show them how you use voice dictation. Building a small community can keep you motivated and open up new ideas.

Dodging the Pitfalls

Over-Reliance on Tools

While assistive tech can be a lifesaver, it's still important to practice key skills. You don't want to lose the ability to type or read basic text entirely. Think of the tools as helpers, not replacements for learning.

Choosing Tools That Don't Fit

If an app's interface feels cluttered or the voice for your text-to-speech grates on your nerves, you're less likely to use it. Try different options until you find one that meshes with your preferences.

Ignoring Setup and Updates

Many tools get better with proper setup—like training speech-to-text to recognize your accent—and regular updates. Skipping these steps might result in subpar performance.

Tool Overload

Using multiple overlapping apps can lead to confusion. If you have tasks scattered across two or three platforms, you could forget which tool houses certain notes. Keep it streamlined, or link apps together if that's an option.

Privacy Concerns

Some apps collect data, including voice recordings or typed text. Check the privacy policy. If you're uneasy, look for alternatives that store data locally or have strong encryption.

Keeping It Neurodivergent-Friendly

Small Steps Over Time

Don't try to master everything at once. Start with a single piece of tech, build confidence, and then explore additional features. This approach avoids sensory overload and frustration.

Visual Cues

If you have memory issues or get distracted, place a sticky note near your computer saying "Remember to turn on TTS!" or "Check the calendar!" Visual cues can keep you from forgetting your new tech helpers.

Pair It with Body Doubling

Some people find it helpful to work alongside a friend or coworker. If you're learning a new assistive tool, do it on a video call with a buddy. They can watch your screen (with permission) and learn along with you. This shared experience might reduce the anxiety of going it alone.

Celebrate Wins

Each time you successfully read a long article using text-to-speech or voice-dictate a big chunk of homework, give yourself a small reward—like a 5-minute music break or a fun sticker on your planner. Recognizing progress keeps motivation high.

The Future of Assistive Tech

Technology continues to evolve. Many apps now include AI features that predict your learning style or suggest personalized study plans. Virtual reality platforms could one day immerse you in learning environments tailored to neurodivergent brains. New hardware might transform everyday objects—like smart glasses that read street signs or instructions aloud. Keeping an eye on emerging tech can be exciting. However, it's also okay to stick with what works. Sometimes the simplest solutions—like a built-in phone dictation tool—do the job just fine. You don't need the latest gadgets if you already have something meeting your needs.

A Toolkit for Independence

Assistive technology isn't just about convenience—it's about unlocking your full potential. For some, it's the difference between staring at a blank screen in frustration and producing a well-written document in half the time.

For others, it's the key to enjoying reading, because now you can listen to text while making dinner or relaxing on the couch. And for many, it's a step toward independence—no more constantly asking for help to read or write something.

Selecting the right tools, learning how to use them, and fitting them into your daily routine can make a world of difference if you've struggled with reading and writing tasks in the past.

You don't have to memorize every detail. Start small, try one or two features, and expand as you get comfortable. Over time, you'll figure out which apps or devices truly support your goals and which ones aren't worth the hassle. The best part is that assistive tech often levels the playing field. It allows those with atypical brains to shine in school, the workplace, or personal hobbies—areas where they might have been held back by tedious reading or writing processes.

By removing barriers, these tools give you the chance to focus on your talents and creativity rather than getting stuck on basic mechanics. They help turn daily challenges into tasks you can handle with confidence.

As you explore different options, keep an open mind. Something that seems awkward on day one might become second nature by day ten. Ask for feedback from friends or mentors, and don't shy away from testing new tools now and then.

Ultimately, assistive technology is about giving yourself more freedom— freedom to learn, express, and thrive without being held back by obstacles that tech can solve. So go ahead, check out that speech-to-text feature, install a text-to-speech plugin, or sign up for a task management app.

With each step, you're crafting a world where reading and writing feel less like chores and more like gateways to your success. And in the end, that's what assistive technology is all about: **helping you live and learn on your terms.**

5

Positive Affirmations

Imagine starting your day with a mental soundtrack that cheers you on. You wake up, stretch, look at yourself in the mirror, and follow the advice of Dax Shepard to his daughter. You say, "I'm a bad b*tch, and I'm gonna f*ck this day up!" As simple as that sounds, it can spark a brighter mood and direct your focus toward what you can achieve.

These short, uplifting statements—often called "affirmations"—may seem too good to be true, but they can have a real impact on how you view your abilities and approach your tasks. In this chapter, we'll talk about how positive affirmations work, why they matter for motivation, and ways to use them for consistent productivity, especially if you have a neurodivergent mind that needs extra encouragement.

What Are Positive Affirmations?

Positive affirmations are short, supportive sentences that highlight your strengths or goals. They serve as quick reminders that you have the power to handle challenges. Think of them as verbal prompts that shift your mindset from worry or self-doubt to optimism. Instead of saying, "I'll never finish this," you tell yourself, "I take things one step at a time." Even though the words are simple, they can change the tone of your day. They're not magic spells, but they do guide your thinking away from negativity and help you notice what's possible.

Why They Work

Research in psychology suggests that when we repeat encouraging phrases, we're more likely to stay calm under pressure and maintain a can-do attitude. Picture an athlete before a big game. They might say, "I've trained hard. I am focused. I will perform on the level only I can." This routine will calm nerves and sharpen the mind. The same idea applies to everyday tasks. Whether you're studying, writing a paper, or trying to organize your schedule, a quick, positive reminder can center your thoughts on progress rather than setbacks.

A Tool for All, Especially Neurodivergent Brains

Anyone can benefit from affirmations, but people with ADHD, autism, or other neurodivergent conditions often battle waves of self-doubt or scattered thinking which rise to the level neurotypical minds don't. Sometimes the world feels overwhelming, and it's easy to get stuck in negative self-talk like, "I can't do this," or "I'm always behind." Positive affirmations interrupt that loop and nudge you back toward a steadier mindset. They act like a supportive friend who's always on your side, whispering, "You've got this."

Affirmations and the Brain

Rewiring Thought Patterns

It's not that you chant a magic phrase and all obstacles disappear. However, each time you repeat a positive statement, you're reinforcing a certain way of thinking. Over days and weeks, that thinking style can become natural. Instead of defaulting to "I'm a failure when I make mistakes," you might start to say, "I learn from my mistakes and grow stronger." You are changing the neuropathways of your mind.

Self-Efficacy Boost

Affirmations help build self-efficacy, which is your belief in your ability to succeed. A strong sense of self-efficacy is tied to better motivation and a greater willingness to tackle tough tasks. If you think you can, you're more likely to try harder, bounce back from errors, and carry on until you reach your goal.

A Cushion for Stress

Stress can creep in when you're unsure of yourself or feeling overwhelmed by deadlines. A simple phrase like, "I know what needs to be done and how to do it," can act as a mental shield. While it won't fix every problem, it cushions your stress reaction, reminding you that you have some control.

Creating Your Affirmations

Keep Them Short

A good rule of thumb is to use statements that are easy to remember and repeat. "I am focused," "I am capable," or "I adapt to anything." Short sentences stick in your mind and pop up when you need them, rather than fading away under daily chaos.

Make Them Personal

General phrases might help at times, but affirmations that match your goals or struggles will resonate more. If you're a student worried about exams, try: "I learn new information easily." If you're stepping into a leadership role, "I guide others with confidence and empathy" could be your go-to statement.

Choose a Present-Tense Voice

Saying "I will be confident" can sound like it's still in the future. "I am confident" brings the mindset into the present moment, nudging your brain to act like it's already true. Even if you don't feel super confident yet, the present tense can encourage growth in that direction.

Example Affirmations

- "I handle change with steady focus."
- "I bring unique skills to every challenge I face."
- "I improve each day."

Practical Affirmation Habits

Morning Ritual

Set aside one to two minutes each morning to recite your affirmations out loud or in your head. Some people like to stand in front of the mirror and say them. Others prefer a quiet moment in bed or while making coffee. This brief activity can color your entire day with a more confident outlook.

Post-It Reminders

Write your affirmations on sticky notes (yep, here they are again) and place them where you'll see them: bathroom mirrors, computer screens, or notebooks. That's an easy way to keep them fresh in your mind. If a note has been in the same spot for weeks and you barely notice it anymore, move it or change the color so it catches your eye again.

Phone Notifications

Set an alarm or notification on your phone that displays an affirmation a few times a day. For example, at 2 p.m., you might get a popup saying, "Rest when you need it." At 5 p.m., a reminder might say, "No matter the size, progress is progress."

Pair Them with Existing Habits

Linking affirmations to habits you already have can embed them deeper. For instance, each time you open your calendar app, read a specific affirmation about time management. Or every time you sit down for a meal, mentally recite one about self-care and relaxation.

How Affirmations Boost Productivity

Shifting from Negative to Constructive Self-Talk

Neurodivergent individuals can get tangled in critical self-talk. Maybe you started a project but can't seem to focus, and the voice in your head says, "You're hopeless at this." Switching to an affirmation—like, "I am finishing this. Just go step by step"—interrupts that loop. This new voice encourages you to keep going, even if you move slower than you hoped.

Improving Resilience

Productivity isn't just about knocking tasks off a list. It's also about bouncing back when things go wrong. Affirmations act like mental anchors. When you face a setback, you lean on the idea that "I adapt and find solutions." This keeps frustration from spiraling out of control and shortens the time you spend in a slump.

Encouraging Follow-Through

Affirmations set the stage for consistent action. When you start believing you can handle a task, you're more likely to see it through. You stop giving up at the first hurdle because, deep down, you trust yourself to figure it out. That sense of trust can be the difference between an abandoned project and a completed one.

Small Rewards for Affirmation Practice

Many people find it helpful to reward themselves for keeping up with affirmations. It could be a sticker in a journal each day you repeat them, or a quick treat at the end of the week if you kept track of your affirmations daily. These small rewards reinforce the habit until it becomes second nature.

Addressing Skepticism

"Aren't Affirmations Just Wishful Thinking?"

It's okay to be skeptical. Some people imagine that repeating a phrase is like telling yourself a fairy tale. But affirmations aren't about denying reality. They're about choosing a helpful perspective. If you normally think, "I'll fail anyway," that mindset can block you from trying. Shifting to a supportive phrase doesn't guarantee success, but it opens you up to making an honest attempt.

"What If I Don't Believe My Own Words?"

At first, you might feel silly or fake reciting affirmations that don't match your current feelings. That's normal. The trick is consistency. The more you practice, the more your mind warms up to the idea. It's like learning a new language—you might trip over the words initially, but you gain fluency with time. In the meantime, try focusing on aspects of the phrase you can believe.

For example, if "I am organized" feels too big a stretch, start with "I am learning to plan my tasks better."

Affirmations for The ND Mind

Tailor to Your Challenges

If organization is a constant headache, build your statement around that. If emotional regulation is tough, use something that reminds you to breathe and stay calm. Specific affirmations work better than generic ones. Think about what holds you back. If it's procrastination, "Any step forward is a good step" can help you begin.

Use Humor and Fun

Not all affirmations need to be serious. Sometimes a playful phrase makes it more memorable and less forced. For instance, "I'm the boss of my inbox" or "I tackle clutter like a superhero." Adding humor can spark a smile, which can also lift your mood.

Pair with Another Sensory Element

If reading words isn't enough, combine them with something visual or tactile. Maybe you draw a simple symbol next to your affirmation—a sun, star, or heart—that represents hope. Or keep a small object in your pocket that you associate with positive energy. Every time you touch it, you recall your affirmation.

Mindful Moments

Affirmations can blend well with mindfulness. While you breathe in and out, mentally repeat your chosen phrase. Feel the rhythm of your breath aligning with the words. This approach can be calming and help the statement sink deeper into your mind.

Dodge the Drama with Affirmations

Too Many Phrases

If you try to adopt ten new affirmations at once, you might get lost or forget half of them. Start small—one or two statements that you can focus on for a week or two. Once they feel natural, add another one.

Being Too Vague

"I am awesome" might sound positive, but it's not specific enough to combat a real concern. Narrow it down: "I find creative solutions to any problem" or "I communicate clearly with others." Target your actual needs or fears.

Inconsistent Practice

Affirmations work best with regular use. If you only try them once in a while, they're easy to forget. Make them part of a daily routine, whether it's morning coffee or bedtime reflection. Consistency cements the new outlook.

Forgetting to Tie Action to Words

Affirmations can boost your mindset, but you still need to follow through with action. If your affirmation is about improving study habits, also set up a study plan or use productivity apps. The statements support you, but the actions move you forward.

Using Affirmations as a Mask

Don't ignore genuine struggles or mental health concerns by covering them with "Everything is fine." If deeper issues exist—like depression or severe anxiety—affirmations can be one part of a broader self-care plan that may include lifestyle changes, therapy, and sometimes medication. A balanced approach often works best.

Affirmations and Group Support

Sharing with Friends or Family

Sometimes speaking affirmations aloud together can strengthen their effect. If you have a supportive friend or family member, consider sharing your favorite phrases. Ask them to remind you of those statements when you seem discouraged. This shared practice can create a bond and keep you accountable.

Online Communities

Forums and social media groups exist where people post daily affirmations or positivity challenges (Including *The ND Mind*). Joining one can motivate you to craft or refine your statements. You also gain a sense of community—others are on the same journey, and you can cheer each other on.

Affirmations as an Ongoing Practice

Regular Check-Ins

Like I said earlier, affirmations aren't a one-time event. Schedule check-ins (maybe weekly, monthly, etc.) to review which statements still resonate. Sometimes your focus shifts. Perhaps you once struggled with confidence, but now your challenge is keeping up the momentum. Update your affirmations to match new goals.

Celebrate Your Growth

Each time you see progress, **acknowledge your progress**. If you used to freeze when facing a new project but now dive in with curiosity, notice that shift. Affirmations play a role in this growth, so take a moment to appreciate how far you've come.

Pairing with Other Hacks

Positive affirmations combine nicely with other productivity techniques, such as body breaks, visual reminders, or assistive technology. For example, if you use a digital planner, add a motivational phrase at the top. Or if you have color-coded sticky notes, write a brief affirmation on each color. This layered approach can make your productivity system feel more encouraging.

A Future Driven by Self-Belief

Positive affirmations aren't a substitute for hard work or skill-building. They're like the wind in your sails, supporting and guiding you as you navigate daily life. For neurodivergent minds that often wrestle with doubt or scattered focus, affirmations can be a gentle anchor in busy waters.

The real payoff is the mindset shift that forms over time. Instead of labeling yourself as "someone who can't organize tasks," you become "someone who is managing tasks better each day." That small change in perspective can keep you motivated when challenges appear. Affirmations can remind you that you hold the power to keep growing, adapting, and achieving.

So, why not start today? Pick one affirmation that calls out to you. Maybe it's "I handle whatever the day brings" or "I finish what I begin." Say it or write it in a place you'll see it often. As you move through your tasks, keep these words close at hand. Over time, you'll likely notice you're less weighed down by self-criticism and more fueled by self-encouragement.

You're taking real steps toward a mindset that's ready to learn, persevere, and celebrate every win—even the small ones.

6

Celebrate Small Wins

Think about the last time you accomplished something. Maybe you finished a tedious chore or managed to stay focused for a solid half-hour on a project. How did you mark that success? Did you pause for a moment of pride, or did you rush to the next task? For many of us—especially those of us with neurodivergent minds—celebrating small wins often falls by the wayside. We zoom from one hurdle to the next without giving ourselves any credit.

But these little celebrations can add up in a big way, fueling motivation and lifting our self-esteem. This chapter delves into why acknowledging small victories matters and offers practical ways to track and reflect on achievements, no matter how modest they may seem.

Why Small Wins Are a Big Deal

A Boost for the Brain

Our brains love success. Even tiny victories can spark a release of dopamine, the feel-good chemical associated with reward and motivation. Think of a video game: you complete a level, and you get a flashy "Congratulations!" message, maybe some coins or a rising point tally. That feedback keeps you playing.

In real life, small wins can generate that same sense of progress. If you ignore those small wins, you miss the mental boost they provide. Neurodivergent people, who may already struggle with consistent motivation, can benefit even more from taking note of each positive step.

Building Momentum

Imagine that every small win is like a log on a fire. One log might not seem like much, but keep stacking them, and soon you have a roaring blaze. Each achievement, whether it's finishing a short reading assignment or cleaning off your desk, adds to your growing sense of momentum. Momentum makes it easier to tackle bigger goals because you're no longer staring at a mountain of undone tasks—you're standing on top of a pile of completed ones.

Charge the Battery

Picture a friend who tries to run a marathon without ever celebrating a shorter run. They run three miles, then five miles, and never give themselves a pat on the back. By the time they get to the half-marathon, they're too exhausted—mentally more than physically.

It's like they forgot to charge their mental batteries along the way. That's why celebrating small achievements can feel like plugging in your phone before it hits zero percent. You wouldn't let your phone die on you, right?

The Psychology Behind Celebrations

Positive Reinforcement

In behavioral psychology, positive reinforcement means you reward a behavior so it's more likely to happen again. If you treat yourself to something pleasant each time you finish a mini-project, your brain starts linking "completing tasks" with "good vibes." Over time, you want that good feeling again. This is how celebrating small wins can gradually shift your mindset from dreading tasks to seeing them as opportunities for small bursts of happiness.

Fighting Negative Self-Talk

Neurodivergent individuals might wrestle with thoughts like, "I'm always behind," or "I can't focus like everyone else." By celebrating small wins, you create factual evidence that contradicts that negativity. Instead of telling yourself, "I never get anything done," you can point to actual items checked off your list. Every time you mark a small success, you chip away at that inner voice claiming you can't achieve your goals. It's like presenting a counter-argument to self-doubt.

The Snowball Effect

Let's say you celebrate finishing a chapter of your book. The good mood from that celebration might help you tackle writing a summary of the chapter. After that, you might feel spurred to prepare for your next assignment. Each little success nudges you toward another. The opposite is also true: if you never pause to note your progress, it's easy to feel like you're in a never-ending grind.

Ways to Mark Each Success

Checklists and Crossing Things Off

A classic approach is making a to-do list and crossing off tasks as you complete them. The physical action of drawing a line or ticking a checkbox can be surprisingly satisfying. Some people love digital apps for this—others prefer a simple piece of paper. If you have ADHD or struggle with scattered thoughts, a dedicated to-do list can be an anchor. Each time you strike out a task (even if you added a task you've already done just so you can cross it off first), you give yourself a mini high-five. That quick jolt of "Yes, I did something!" might be all you need to keep rolling.

Journaling or "Success Logs"

Another method is to keep a small notebook or digital journal where you record daily achievements. These can be modest, like "Stayed focused for 15 minutes without checking my phone" or "Remembered to water the plants." Over time, you'll gather a record of personal victories. On days when you feel like you haven't done anything right, flipping through past entries can remind you of your capacity for success.

Sticker Charts and Visual Trackers

Stickers aren't just for kids. Many adults find them oddly motivating. Place a colorful sticker on a chart (or even on a piece of paper taped to the wall) every time you complete a step. The visual progression can be encouraging. Likewise, digital habit-tracking apps often show streaks or progress bars. Watching your streak grow might spark enough excitement to keep you going. Think of it like playing a game where every day you "level up" a little more.

Share It with Someone

If you're comfortable, tell a friend or family member each time you hit a small milestone. Maybe you text them a quick "I did it!" message. Some people even form small accountability groups where everyone shares daily progress. Receiving a thumbs-up or "Way to go!" can reinforce that sense of accomplishment. It also helps you realize that your achievements matter, even if they look small on paper.

Take a Moment of Rest

Celebrations don't always have to be high-energy. Sometimes the best reward is a moment of relaxation—like sitting quietly with a cup of tea, letting yourself bask in the feeling of "I completed something." For those who constantly jump to the next task, this forced pause can be a refreshing way to acknowledge a job well done.

Tracking and Reflecting

Daily Reflection Time

Set aside a few minutes, either at the start or end of your day, to reflect on what you accomplished. Ask yourself, "Which tasks did I finish?" and "What did I learn from that process?" Write down your answers or speak them out loud if writing feels tedious. This small ritual can turn celebrating into a daily habit.

Example Prompt

- What was one thing I did today that moved me closer to my goals?
    - What is one thing I learned about my focus or energy levels?
    - How can I build on today's success tomorrow?

Weekly or Monthly Overviews

A longer view can help you spot bigger patterns. Maybe at the end of each week, you flip through your success logs or to-do lists. Look for trends: which tasks pop up often? Do you have any repeated small wins that indicate a growing strength? A monthly review can be more general—like noticing that you consistently managed morning routines without feeling frazzled. These overviews help you see your long-term progress and reinforce the idea that small steps truly add up.

Visual Boards

For a more creative approach, you might consider making a "victory board." This can be physical (like a bulletin board) or digital (like a Trello board). Post something that represents each success—a photo, a note, or a mini report.

Over time, the board becomes a collage of your achievements, reminding you of the journey you're on.

Journaling with a Twist

If you're into writing, try short journaling prompts like "Win of the Day" or "Progress I'm Proud Of." Keep it brief, maybe two or three sentences. If you have ADHD and dread writing longer entries, set a timer for one minute. When time's up, you stop. This time limit can make journaling feel more approachable. Over a month, you'll have 30 short blurbs celebrating your wins.

How Celebrations Help

Encouraging Consistency

One challenge for neurodivergent people is sticking with routines or focusing over time. Celebrating small wins builds positive feedback into your day, making routines more enjoyable. Instead of feeling like you're on a never-ending treadmill, you get little breaks of excitement or relief.

Self-Worth and Identity

Over time, consistent celebration can reshape how you view yourself. Instead of saying, "I'm the person who can't keep up," you start to think, "I'm someone who knocks out a step or two each day and sees results." These subtle changes in self-identity can boost your willingness to try new things or take on bigger challenges.

Reducing Burnout

It's easy to burn out when every day feels like drudgery. Celebrations inject a dose of fun and reward, balancing out the mental strain. Think of it like giving your brain a cookie (metaphorically, or literally if you prefer) after it works hard. By weaving tiny celebrations into daily life, you avoid that bleak feeling of "What am I even doing all this for?"

Adjusting to Your Own Pace

Neurodivergent individuals often compare themselves to others, feeling inadequate if they move more slowly or need different structures. Celebrating your wins, no matter their size, reminds you that your pace is valid. A single step forward might be a significant feat in your context, and that's worth cheering about.

Getting Through the Roadblocks

Forgetting to Celebrate

It's easy to get so wrapped up in doing stuff that you skip the celebration part. A workaround is to tie celebrations to something you already do. For instance, if you use a planner or habit tracker, include a "Celebrate Step" after you check off an item. Or set an alarm that says, "Find one thing to celebrate right now."

Downplaying Your Wins

Some people shrug off their achievements as "no big deal." If this sounds like you, remember that success is relative. Maybe someone else can breeze through your task in two minutes, but for you, it's a real challenge. Recognizing that difference is key. If it felt like work, it deserves a small celebration, period.

Overdoing It

Yes, there's a balance to strike. If you celebrate by taking an hour-long break every time you spend five minutes on a task, you might lose track of the bigger picture. Keep rewards fun but proportionate. For example, a two-minute dance party is a perfect little break—celebratory, but not so large that you derail your entire day.

Comparing Celebrations

You might see a friend's fancy bullet journal with elaborate calligraphy for marking wins and think, "I should do that." Then you get overwhelmed and do nothing. Remember that your celebration method can be simple. A quick "Yes, I did it!" can be just as meaningful as an intricate illustration.

Not Updating the System

Over time, you might get bored with your current celebration method. Switch it up! If you've been using stickers, try a paper chain where each link represents a success. Or if you love digital logs, maybe you switch to short video clips celebrating each milestone. Variety keeps the process fresh.

Infusing Fun into Celebrations

Make It Social

Consider small "achievement threads" with friends—like in a group text or on a discord—where each person shares one recent accomplishment. Keep it lighthearted: maybe each share is followed by a GIF of some applause or a funny dance move. It might sound silly, but that's the point! A bit of silliness can make achievement-sharing something you look forward to.

Gamify Your Progress

Pretend your tasks are quests, and each completed task drops "loot." That loot could be a break with your favorite music, a piece of candy, or even just the satisfaction of leveling up a personal progress meter. Some apps let you set up your life as a role-playing game, complete with avatars and experience points for tasks. If that style clicks with you, it can transform mundane chores into playful adventures.

Take a Victory Lap

Sometimes a physical celebration can underline your progress. Do a quick dance, a fist pump, or a mini lap around your home. Movement (there it is again!) can help anchor the sense of triumph in your body. It sounds silly, but physically celebrating can release even more feel-good chemicals. It's like you're telling your brain, "We did it!" loud and clear.

Long-Term Benefits of Celebrating Small Wins

Growing Self-Confidence

Every small achievement you honor contributes to a stronger belief in your capabilities. Over time, you build a bank of evidence that you are indeed someone who gets things done. When bigger challenges arise, you can dip into this "confidence account" and remind yourself you've tackled plenty of tasks before.

Strengthening Resilience

Life throws curve balls. Celebrating small wins won't remove setbacks, but it can make you more resilient. When you're used to cheering yourself on regularly, one slip-up doesn't define your entire week. You know there are always more mini-wins around the corner.

Shaping a Positive Mindset

Habits mold our worldview. If your habit is to acknowledge and appreciate forward movement—even in tiny increments—you're training your mind to see the positives in daily life. This doesn't mean you ignore problems; it means you approach them with a solution-focused, hopeful perspective, rather than a doom-and-gloom lens.

Staying Motivated

Motivation can be slippery, especially for neurodivergent folks who might experience bursts of hyper focus followed by stretches of inertia. By celebrating wins, you're essentially refilling your motivation tank. Each bit of recognition acts like a small top-up, keeping you from running on empty.

Acknowledge Your Progress

Celebrating small wins is more than just patting yourself on the back. It's a method to anchor your progress, build confidence, and keep the fires of motivation burning. Whether you check off tasks on a sticky note, fill out a success log, or do a quick victory dance, the point is to shine a light on what you've accomplished. Too often, we focus on what still needs doing and forget to notice what we've already done.

For neurodivergent minds, who might battle negative self-talk or a constant sense of overwhelm, these little celebrations can be a lifeline. They remind you that every bit counts, that you're moving forward at your own pace, and that your efforts deserve recognition. Over time, these quick "good job" moments rewire your approach to tasks, nudging you toward resilience and self-belief.

So, grab a pen and circle that completed to-do item, draw a bright star next to it, or share your success with a trusted friend. Don't underestimate the power of these small gestures. With each celebration, you're fueling a mindset that understands one simple truth: small wins—when acknowledged—can lead to big transformations. Keep celebrating, keep growing, and watch how those tiny moments of triumph spark a lasting change in how you see yourself and your potential.

II

Time Management and Organization

Time—it's that sneaky magician that disappears faster than the socks from your laundry. For many of us it's not just about losing time, it's about never quite knowing where it went in the first place.

Instead of starting your day hours-deep figuring out if raccoons swim well (they do), this part of the book is about practical, flexible tools for managing your time without stifling your creativity and avoiding the hamster wheel.

7

Color-Coded Task Lists

You just woke up and BAM—your mile-long to-do list is staring you in the face. Maybe it's a plain sheet of paper covered in black ink or a digital list with one line after another. If you're like many of us—especially those with "spicy" minds—this uniform layout can feel overwhelming, making each task blend. Enter color-coded (sensing a theme yet?) task lists: a simple, adaptable strategy that uses bright hues to bring clarity and relief.

In this chapter, we'll look at how color can transform your to-do list from a cluttered mess into a quick-read roadmap. You'll learn why color helps you focus, how to assign hues in ways that make sense, and how to tailor the system to fit your style.

Why Color Works

Breaking Through the Noise

We live in a world filled with constant information and stimulation. A single phone screen can show weather updates, text messages, and ads all at once. In this noisy environment, our brains look for cues to know what to focus on. The color stands out because it naturally grabs our attention. For instance, when you see a neon sign on a busy street; you notice it faster than a dull gray poster. The same principle applies to your to-do list. Splashes of color break through the monotony, offering your eyes a clear place to land.

Quick Visual Sorting

Think of color as a "label" you don't need to read. When you see something in red, you might instantly think, "urgent" or "important." If you spot a calming blue, maybe it signals "creative tasks" or "low priority." This immediate recognition cuts down on the time spent scanning and re-scanning your list, freeing your mind for actual work. For those with ADHD or other neurodivergent traits, any system that reduces the need for repeated reading can be a serious time—and mental-processing—saver.

Emotional Boost

Colors can also influence mood—think about how certain shades make you feel. Warm colors like yellow or orange can energize, while greens and blues might soothe. Including color in your task management isn't just about organization; it can also subtly shift how you feel about your responsibilities. For example, using a bright yellow for smaller tasks might make them seem more manageable. Or a cool green for personal projects might give you a sense of calm. When you pick colors that you like, your to-do list can become less of a chore and more of a friendly reminder.

The Science of Overwhelm (and How Color Helps)

Visual Overload

When everything on a list looks the same, your brain has to rely on text alone to figure out what matters most. This can lead to what some call "analysis paralysis"—you're so busy sorting through words that you never dive into the tasks themselves. For neurodivergent folks, that sense of overwhelm can come on fast. You might try reading your list multiple times, losing momentum with each pass. Color-coded sections act like road signs that say,

"Stop here," or "Check this first," cutting through the clutter.

Task Chunking

Many productivity experts talk about "chunking" tasks, or breaking them into manageable pieces. Color coding works hand in hand with chunking. You can group similar tasks—like errands or phone calls—under one color so they feel like a single batch. This approach helps your brain see patterns, such as "All my red tasks are phone-related; let's knock them out in one go." (This is a great strategy for those of us who have great disdain for making phone calls.) By organizing tasks into color-coded clusters, you save mental energy. Instead of toggling between random items, you handle one category at a time.

Fighting Fatigue

It's exhausting to rely purely on words. Neuroscientists point out that our brains developed to respond quickly to visual cues. If you're already prone to mental fatigue (common in ADHD or autism), giving your eyes and brain an easier path can keep you from burning out. Imagine scanning your list and seeing "green means financial tasks," so you instantly know which tasks to tackle if you're focusing on money-related items that day. You avoid wading through everything else.

Choosing Your Color Scheme

Simple vs. Rainbow

There's no universal rule on how many colors you should use. Some people thrive with a rainbow approach—red, orange, yellow, green, blue, purple—giving each color a meaning. Others prefer two or three main hues to keep it simpler. Too many colors can turn into visual noise if you're not careful. Start small, see what works, then add more if you need them.

Personal Preferences

Pick colors that resonate with you. If orange feels jarring or overstimulating, skip it. If you adore purple, find a job for that color, even if it's just to label "self-care" tasks. Personal preference is key; you're more likely to use the system if the colors make sense and don't irritate you. Remember, this is your list, so it should please your eyes.

Assigning Meaning

One common approach is to link each color with a specific category. For instance, red for urgent tasks, blue for family responsibilities, green for work projects, and yellow for personal errands. Another method is to match colors with urgency levels—red for "must do today," orange for "do this week," and blue for "long-term projects." Some folks combine categories and urgency, using shades of a single color to show how soon a category's tasks need to be done. For instance, light green for low-priority finance tasks, and dark green for urgent finance tasks.

Quick Tips for Color Assignment

- **Red or orange:** Urgent items, deadlines, or anything that needs immediate attention.
- **Yellow or green:** Moderately important tasks—things that need to be done soon but aren't on fire yet (and we won't let them get there, right?).
- **Blue or purple:** Longer-term or creative projects that can wait if needed.
- **Pink or pastel hues:** Personal or fun tasks that you don't want to forget but aren't super critical.

Color-Coding Tools and Techniques

Physical Lists and Planners

If you love the tactile feel of pen and paper, you can use colored pens, highlighters, or sticky notes. For instance, write each category of tasks with a different colored pen. Or keep a black pen for writing tasks and use a highlighter to mark each item's category. Colored sticky notes can also double as movable tasks, handy if you like rearranging your list without rewriting everything.

Pro Tip: Don't worry about perfect handwriting or neatness. The main point is to have quick visual markers. A sloppy highlight is better than no highlight if it helps you spot a priority at a glance.

Digital Options

Fans of digital productivity tools have plenty of color-coding features at their fingertips. Apps like Trello, Asana, and Notion let you assign colored labels or tags to tasks. You can also change the background color of each note or card. Some people go the extra mile by creating an entire color-coded folder system on their computer or email, ensuring that work documents might be in one color-coded folder, personal finance in another, and so forth.

Pro Tip: If you're using a digital tool, explore whether it lets you filter tasks by color. That way, you can click a button and instantly see only your "red" tasks (urgent) or "blue" tasks (creative projects).

Hybrid Approaches

You don't have to pick between paper and digital. Perhaps you keep a main list on an app that color-codes broad categories, but you also use physical sticky notes for daily tasks. Some find it helpful to do big-picture planning digitally—where color labels are easily changed—then copy each day's tasks onto a paper list in a color-coded pen. Flexibility is the key. Use what feels natural to you.

Putting Color Coding into Practice

Step 1: Brain Dump

Start by listing out all your tasks, ignoring color for the moment. This step ensures you don't miss anything. If your mind feels scattered, write everything down, from "call the dentist" to "research new job ideas."

Step 2: Sort into Categories or Urgency

Next, group tasks into clusters. You might find four main groups: work, home, personal development, and errands. Or if you prefer urgency-based sorting, you might group tasks into "do today," "do this week," and "do eventually."

Step 3: Assign Colors

Take your chosen categories (or urgency levels) and pair them with specific colors. For instance, if you have four groups, pick four colors you enjoy. If you're going the urgency route, decide which color signals immediate tasks and which color signals "on hold."

Step 4: Label or Highlight

Now, label each task with the appropriate color. If you're digital, open the app and assign each item a colored tag or label. If you're on paper, use a highlighter or colored pen. Try not to overthink; the goal is clarity, not artistic perfection.

Step 5: Review and Adjust

Take a moment to scan your newly color-coded list. Does it make sense at a glance? If certain colors look too similar, you might swap them out. If you realize you have too many categories, combine a few. The idea is to find that sweet spot where your list is visually easy to parse without drowning in a rainbow overload.

Benefits for Neurodivergent Minds

Reduced Overwhelm

By chunking your tasks into color-coded sections, you tame that "all tasks are equally demanding" feeling. You can ignore the green tasks if you're in "urgent mode" and need to focus on red. This helps you dive into your day with more calm and less anxiety.

Faster Decision-Making

Many neurodivergent individuals face decision fatigue, where even small choices feel exhausting. Color coding handles a big slice of that work for you. When you're ready to focus on, say, your top priorities, you just look at the red tasks first. No more asking yourself three times, "Which one should I do now?"

Consistent Engagement

If your mind thrives on variety, color-coded lists can keep you engaged. Switching from red tasks to green tasks feels like a mini-shift in focus, which can refresh your attention. On the flip side, if you do better with routine, you can stick to one color category at a time, grouping similar tasks for uninterrupted flow.

Whack-a-mole

Handling tasks often feels like a game of whack-a-mole, especially for those with ADHD or anxiety. Color coding brings a sense of order you can see right in front of you. It provides a feeling that you're steering the ship rather than reacting to everything at once.

Steer Clear of Color Coding Chaos

Too Many Colors

It's easy to get excited and assign a different color to each type of task. Soon, you might have a list that looks like a bag of Skittles, and your brain doesn't know what to do with the chaos.

Solution: Start with three or four main colors at most. You can always add more later if you find a real need.

Color Overload

If certain shades feel harsh on your eyes or cause sensory overload, you might shy away from using the system.

Solution: Choose softer pastel tones or colors you find calming. There's no rule saying "urgent tasks" must be a blaring red if that stresses you out. Maybe a deeper shade of orange will do the trick.

Inconsistent Use

Color coding only helps if you keep doing it. If you color-code one day and ignore it the next, tasks slip back into a single big blob.

Solution: Make color-coding part of your routine. If you journal every night or plan every morning, that's the time to add or update color labels. Think of it as a quick, must-do step—like brushing your teeth.

Lack of Clarity

You might forget why you chose certain colors. Purple tasks? Were they errands or creative projects?

Solution: Keep a small legend or key somewhere visible. Even a note on your desk. Over time, you'll memorize it, but the key will save you in the early weeks.

Missing the Big Picture

Color coding helps with immediate scanning, but you might forget to consider long-term or bigger goals.

Solution: Combine color-coding with a weekly or monthly review of your progress. Zoom out and see which categories got the most attention. Did you neglect self-care tasks (purple) for too long? Adjust accordingly.

Adding Subtle Fun to the Process

Without drawing too much attention to it, sprinkling a bit of humor or playfulness can keep the color-coding habit appealing:

- **Color Names:** Instead of calling it just "red," label it in your mind as "Dragon's Flame," or rename "blue" as "Ocean Adventure." It's a private joke that makes tasks slightly more interesting.
- **Stickers or Emojis:** Alongside or instead of a color highlight, place a small sticker or relevant emoji. Maybe a check-mark for completed tasks, a star for tasks you're excited about, and so forth.
- **Theme Days:** If you're feeling particularly creative, you might assign a day of the week to a color. For instance, "Mondays are Blue Days" for your long-term project tasks. Remember, the main goal is to reduce stress, so keep things fun without adding unnecessary complexity.

When to Review and Revise Your System

Regular Assessments

It's a good idea to look over your color-coding system at the end of each week. Ask yourself, "Is this helping me focus or adding confusion?" If you find you're constantly mixing up certain colors, switch them. If a category you created no longer fits your life, merge it with another.

Life Changes

Major life events—like a new job, moving to a new city, or starting a family—might shift your priorities. When these changes happen, your categories might need an overhaul. Don't be afraid to scrap the old color scheme and invent a fresh one more in tune with your new responsibilities.

Burnout Signs

If the color-coding itself feels like a chore—if you dread picking up that red pen—it might be time for a break or a simpler system. Productivity hacks should make life smoother, not weigh you down. You can always return to color coding once your schedule cools off.

Tying It All Together

Color-coded task lists are like personalized traffic lights for your daily life. They tell your brain "stop right here, do this first" or "proceed at your leisure." By dividing tasks into visual categories, you cut down on mental clutter and pave the way for quicker decision-making. Especially for neurodivergent minds, this method can bridge the gap between endless to-dos and a system that feels friendlier and more inviting. **You don't have to master color coding overnight.**

Experiment with a couple of colors, see how your mind responds, and build from there. Keep it flexible, tweak it as your life changes, and don't be afraid to inject small doses of humor to keep things fresh. Over time, you might find that your once intimidating list of tasks is now a brighter, more organized road map—and that a little splash of color can go a long way in guiding you to the finish line.

8

Micro-Tasks

Visualize a large puzzle spread out on a table with hundreds of pieces. At first glance, all the little pieces might overwhelm you. Where do you begin? Yet the moment you focus on just one section (I start with the edges) it feels more doable. That's the idea behind micro-tasks: breaking big projects into tiny steps so they seem less intimidating.

For many with cognitive differences, who can easily get lost in details or overwhelmed by sheer scope, micro-tasks can be a breath of fresh air. This chapter explores how these small, bite-sized actions can help you keep a steady pace, stay motivated, and avoid the dreaded sinkhole of procrastination.

Why Micro-Tasks Matter

Tackling the Overwhelm

Big projects can feel like staring at a mountain from its base, asking yourself, "How on earth will I ever get to the top?" The brain might freeze, especially if you struggle with focus or get anxious about complicated tasks. Micro-tasks offer a solution: instead of trying to conquer the entire mountain, you aim for the next small ledge. These tiny steps build confidence because each little push gets you visibly closer to the goal.

Instant Gratification

As we've talked about in some of the earlier tips, we're wired to enjoy quick wins. Each time you check off a small step—like drafting a single paragraph or collecting the materials you need—you get a mini jolt of accomplishment. This dopamine hit can be particularly helpful for those who find it hard to stay on track for extended periods. The more micro-tasks you complete, the more motivated you feel to keep going.

Easier Planning

Smaller tasks are naturally simpler to schedule. Rather than blocking off three hours for "Work on the business plan," you might plan 20 minutes for "Write elevator pitch" or 10 minutes for "Outline revenue streams." This bite-sized approach blends well with busy schedules or fluctuating energy levels. If you have a random spare 15 minutes in your day, you can knock out one micro-task rather than waiting for a huge chunk of free time that might never come.

The Science of Breaking Things Down

"Chunking" is a term psychologists use to describe how people group information to remember it more effectively. Think of a phone number— divided into smaller groups of digits, it's easier to recall. This principle applies to tasks too. A big, vague item like "Write a research paper" can be mentally exhausting. Splitting it into specific steps—"Pick a topic," "Gather five sources," "Draft an outline," and so on—makes it less of a brain strain. You're more likely to remember and act on each step because your mind recognizes these chunks as manageable pieces.

Lowering the Activation Barrier

In physics, an "activation barrier" is the energy needed to start a chemical reaction. In our daily lives, a psychological activation barrier might be the hurdle you have to clear before beginning any task. When steps are enormous, that barrier looks huge. With micro-tasks, you reduce the startup energy needed. It's simpler to get going on a five-minute job than a multi-hour project. Once you've begun, momentum often carries you forward.

Cognitive Benefits

Many neurodivergent individuals find multi-step planning difficult because it demands working memory and executive function. Breaking tasks down gives your brain smaller packets of information to process, reducing the load. You no longer have to juggle every detail at once; you can address them one at a time.

Breaking Down the Micro-Tasks

Define Your End Goal

Start by clearly stating what you want to achieve. That could be "Complete marketing presentation," "Organize my bedroom closet," or "Learn basic knitting." Having a clear endpoint gives you something tangible to work toward. If the project is still fuzzy, refine it until you can picture what "done" looks like.

List Major Milestones

Identify the main checkpoints or phases in this project. For a marketing presentation, maybe you have "Research data," "Create slides," and "Rehearse." For a closet reorganization, your milestones might be "Sort clothes," "Store seasonal items," and "Donate unwanted items." These larger chunks act like pillars that support the entire project.

Convert Each Milestone into Mini-Steps

Drill down into each milestone. For "Research data," your micro-tasks could be:

1. Identify three sources.
2. Collect relevant stats.
3. Compile into a single document.
4. Double-check for accuracy.

Try to keep each micro-task to a size you could do in 10-30 minutes max. **If something will take an hour or more, consider slicing it further.**

Sequence the Steps

Some tasks must happen in order. For example, you can't compile stats before identifying sources. Other tasks are flexible, so you can choose what feels right in the moment. If strict sequencing feels too rigid, just note any critical order—like needing to buy paint before painting a wall—and let the rest be fluid.

Assign Time Estimates

Estimate how long each micro-task will take. Accuracy isn't crucial; you just want a ballpark figure. Having a rough time estimate helps you decide when to tackle it. If you have only 10 minutes, pick a quick one. If you have an hour, you can handle a slightly bigger chunk.

Maintaining Momentum

The Two-Minute Rule

If you see a micro-task that will take less than two minutes, do it immediately. This approach works well for everyday chores or small bits of a project that might otherwise linger. Think of it like picking up a stray sock on the floor—it's faster to handle it right away than to plan a whole day of sock-picking.

Timed Work Sessions

Neurodivergent minds often respond well to time-blocking methods like the Pomodoro Technique, where you work in short, focused bursts (e.g., 25 minutes) followed by a quick break. Apply this to micro-tasks by allocating a single Pomodoro to finishing a couple of small steps. Because you're dealing with smaller tasks, you get that satisfying feeling of completion multiple times in one work session.

Habit Stacking

Link micro-tasks to routines you already have. For instance, if you're organizing your closet, you might decide, "Each night after I brush my teeth, I'll sort one drawer or fold ten items." By attaching your micro-task to an existing habit, you're less likely to forget or skip it. This technique can be especially powerful if you struggle with consistent follow-through.

Reward Yourself

Everyone likes a pat on the back—even if you're the one giving it. When you check off a micro-task, allow a small moment of celebration. This could be a quick break, a sticker in your planner, or a silent "nice job" in your head. However, keep rewards modest so you don't derail your day with a giant detour every time you complete a tiny step.

Overcoming Common Hurdles

Feeling Like It's Too Slow

You might worry that breaking a project into micro-tasks will drag everything out. The opposite often proves true. When tasks are small, you waste less time avoiding them or battling internal resistance. Completing 10 small tasks can happen faster than psyching yourself up for one giant one.

Forgetting the Overall Goal

It's easy to get lost in the micro-tasks and lose sight of the bigger picture. One fix is to keep your main goal visible—a sticky note on your monitor, a quick note in your planner, or a short phrase typed at the top of your digital list. Glancing at the end goal reminds you why these mini-steps matter.

Inconsistent Follow-Through

Even well-planned micro-tasks can slip if you don't have a system to track them. You might try:

- **A dedicated app** (like Trello or Todoist) to house your mini-steps.
- **Paper lists** split into categories, each day focusing on a few tasks.
- **Alarms** on your phone to nudge you during the day, reminding you of a small step you can tackle.

Over-Categorizing

Some people take micro-tasks to an extreme, creating dozens of steps for even the smallest project. This can lead to "organizational overload." The fix? Find a balance. If you're spending more time labeling tasks than doing them, merge or skip a few steps. Aim for micro-tasks that are helpful, not burdensome.

Balancing Structure and Flexibility

Allow for Spontaneity

Rigidly sticking to a pre-written list of micro-tasks can backfire, especially if you have ADHD and thrive on a sense of novelty. If you get a burst of inspiration, feel free to jump to a task that excites you, even if it's not "next" on the list. The point is to remember: **Progress, not perfection.**

Mix in Variety

If you notice monotony, consider alternating between different projects' micro-tasks. For instance, do a short writing step, then tackle a home chore, and then switch back to writing. This rotating style can keep your mind engaged. Just be careful not to juggle too many different projects at once, or you risk scattering your focus.

Update Your Micro-Tasks

Projects evolve, and so should your micro-tasks. Maybe you realize a certain step is no longer needed or that you need additional steps. Regularly check in—maybe once a week—and adjust. A dynamic list stays relevant, whereas a static one can become outdated and discouraging.

Encouraging a Micro-Task Mindset

Start Your Day with One Tiny Win

Kick off your morning by handling a micro-task that's easy but relevant to a bigger project. This "easy starter" sets a tone for progress. If you have a big report due next week, maybe your micro-task is "Write the report's first sentence." It may sound laughably small, but once you've done it, you're more likely to continue.

Accountability Buddies

Team up with a friend or colleague who also uses micro-tasks. You can share your daily mini-steps and check in on each other's progress. The online group, "The ND Mind" is a great place to find others who will celebrate your wins. You could set up a quick text exchange: "I completed micro-task #2—your turn!" This friendly encouragement can keep you on track.

Celebrate Benchmarks

When you complete a certain number of micro-tasks or finish a milestone, take a moment to celebrate. This could be as simple as savoring a snack, taking a brief walk, or updating a visual tracker. Feeling recognized for each phase helps maintain enthusiasm. If you're the type who loves charts, fill in a box or place a sticker for every micro-task you conquer. Whatever you do, make sure to **Acknowledge Your Progress.**

Things to Avoid

Micromanaging Yourself

Turning everything into a micro-task can sometimes lead to overthinking. If you find yourself labeling "open new document" as a separate task from "type first sentence," you may have gone too far. Keep your micro-steps meaningful.

Drifting into Perfectionism

Small tasks can make you hyper-aware of each detail. If you keep redoing one micro-step to perfect it, you might stall. Practice setting a reasonable limit—like 15 minutes per micro-task—before moving on, even if it's not flawless.

Losing Momentum After One Step

Completing a single micro-task is fantastic, but be wary of stopping too soon if you still have the energy to do more. Sometimes, finishing one small step can open the door to tackling the next one right away. It's okay to ride that wave of motivation when it appears.

Underestimating Transitions

Switching from one micro-task to another might create downtime if you're not careful. Try grouping related tasks so you don't waste energy shifting gears too often. If tasks require similar resources—like research materials—cluster them to avoid repeated setups.

Building a Sustainable Habit

Integrate into Your Planning Routine

Whether you schedule your week on Sunday nights or write daily to-do lists each morning, slip micro-task creation into that process. If you see a giant project looming for Friday, break it into micro-steps at the start of the week. By the time Friday arrives, you'll have already handled half the steps.

Practice and Tweak

As with any new system, micro-tasking requires trial and error. Some steps might still feel too big, while others may seem too trivial. Give yourself a few weeks to settle into a rhythm. Observe what works, discard what doesn't, and refine as you go.

Cycle In and Out

You don't have to live in micro-task mode 24/7. Sometimes you'll be in a flow state, happily working on a bigger chunk. Other times, you'll feel scattered and need to rely on micro-tasks more heavily. Think of it as a tool you can pull out whenever you sense overwhelm creeping in.

Where Micro-Tasks Shine Most

Creative Projects

Writing a book (*I did it for this one!*), painting a mural, or composing a piece of music can seem huge. Breaking the process into small steps—like drafting a single scene or sketching a rough outline—lets you make daily progress without killing the creative spark.

Long-Term Goals

If you're aiming to change your lifestyle—say, improving fitness or learning a new language—micro-tasks can help you maintain consistency. Instead of "go to the gym every day," you might try "do 10 push-ups" or "walk around the block" as a micro-step. Achieving these smaller goals consistently can build a strong habit over time.

Tedious Chores

Whether it's de-cluttering your garage or sorting through endless emails, these chores can feel like bottomless pits. But if you process 10 emails or organize one corner of the garage each day, you'll gradually chip away at the mess.

Big Progress with Small Steps

Micro-tasks are more than a productivity hack; they're a shift in perspective. When you stop seeing your projects as towering mountains and start viewing them as collections of small climbs, you empower yourself to begin. **Each step forward, no matter how small, is a victory.**

Over time, those steps add up—the next thing you know, you've reached the summit. For neurodivergent minds, micro-tasks can be a lifeline, keeping you from feeling crushed by deadlines or sprawling assignments. They feed your brain a steady stream of accomplishments, building confidence and helping you move through your day with greater ease. But even if you're not neurodivergent, this method can spark motivation in a world that often demands multitasking on an epic scale. So, whether you're cleaning out the fridge, writing a novel, or prepping for a big exam, remember that you don't have to do it all at once.

Pick a tiny step, tackle it, and celebrate that mini-win. Then pick another. Eventually, those small strides become a journey worth celebrating. And there's no better proof of progress than seeing how each micro-task, when linked together, can shift you from "I can't possibly finish" to "I'm practically there already."

9

Chunk Your Time

Have you ever noticed how a single hour can feel endless on some days but fly by on others? Or maybe you've sat down for a quick task, only to glance at the clock later and realize you've lost an entire afternoon. This elastic sense of time is especially common for neurodivergent individuals, where your focus can fluctuate and tasks can blur together.

That's where "chunking your time" comes in—a strategy for breaking the day into manageable blocks, each with a set work period and a scheduled break. Think of it as giving your mind clear start and stop signals, so you don't drift into marathon sessions or get trapped in time-wasting spirals. In this chapter, we'll explore how time chunking differs from chunking tasks, how to set up your blocks effectively, and why it can create a sense of control in a world where time can feel slippery.

Why Chunking Time Matters

Start and End Points for Your Brain

In time chunking, you divide your day into shorter blocks—like 30 or 45 minutes—rather than tackling tasks indefinitely. Each block has a defined beginning and an equally definite end. This creates a mental boundary that says, "Focus now," and then, "Stop for a break." For many neurodivergent minds, those boundaries act like guardrails, keeping you from veering off into daydreams or feeling like you have to push through endless hours without rest. When the block starts, you activate "work mode." When it ends, you switch gears to "break mode," letting your mind and body reset.

A Different Kind of Chunking

You might recall from the previous chapter how chunking tasks involves breaking a large project into smaller, bite-sized steps. Time chunking addresses a different angle: instead of slicing the project itself into micro-steps, you slice your available work hours into smaller segments. You still might have a giant to-do list, but now you're not assigning each item a mini-step; you're saying, "For the next 30 minutes, I'll work on tasks A, B, and C—then I'll pause." The focus is on how long you work, not on completing a project from start to finish in one go.

Fighting Time Distortion

Many people—especially those with ADHD and other conditions—experience "time blindness." This means it's easy to lose track of how long you've been working or how much you can realistically get done in a certain timeframe. Time chunking can be revolutionary. When the timer or clock signals that your block is over, you gain an objective marker of passing time. No more guessing, "Have I been at this for an hour or just five minutes?" You have concrete evidence to guide your next moves.

The Basics of Time Chunking

The Pomodoro (or Block) Technique

One popular version of time chunking is the Pomodoro Technique, where you work for 25 minutes and break for 5 minutes, repeating that cycle multiple times. But there's no one-size-fits-all rule. Some people thrive on 25-

minute blocks, while others find 45 minutes hits the sweet spot. Longer blocks—like 60 to 90 minutes—may work if you tend to hyper-focus or have tasks that require deeper immersion. The key is to pick a block length that feels challenging but not exhausting, leaving you enough brainpower to get something done without burning out.

Scheduled Breaks

Time chunking emphasizes breaks as a non-negotiable part of the process. This is different from simply saying, "I'll work until I'm tired." You decide in advance that, after a set number of minutes, you'll stop working—no matter where you are in a task—and rest. Make sure your break relates to the amount of "work time." A 30-minute block could be 25 minutes of working and a 5-minute break, while a 90-minute block would have a 15-minute break. The scheduled pause gives your brain a chance to breathe, reducing the risk of mental fatigue and distractions creeping in because you're simply worn out.

Prioritizing Tasks Within Blocks

While micro-tasking focuses on breaking tasks themselves into tiny pieces, time chunking gives you a container (the block) where you can address multiple tasks or just one big one. Before a block starts, decide which tasks you'll tackle in that window. For instance, you might dedicate a 30-minute block to "answering emails and Slack messages." Or if you need deep focus, you might reserve a 45-minute block for "researching and outlining next week's report." When the block ends, you're free to review your progress, see if you need another block for the same task, or switch to something else.

Cognitively-Atypical Benefits

Clear Boundaries for Focus

Neurodivergent individuals often describe feeling scattered or pulled in many directions. Time chunking provides structure, saying, "For these 30 minutes, you're doing only this set of tasks." This mental fence can help prevent random wanderings into social media or other distractions because you know you'll get a break soon. Having a defined endpoint makes it easier to say, "I can hold off on checking my phone until this block is done."

Built-In Breaks That Prevent Overwhelm

It's easy to fall into the trap of working for hours on end, especially if you hyper-focus. While hyper-focus can be productive, it can also lead to burnout if you don't come up for air. Time chunking ensures regular pauses, so you don't accidentally spiral into a five-hour session without hydration or rest. These breaks are particularly valuable if you struggle with executive functioning—remembering to stand up, drink water, or even use the restroom.

Flexible for Different Task Types

Tasks vary widely—some need deep, extended focus (like writing a complex report), while others benefit from quick bursts of attention (like sorting emails). You can customize block lengths to match your style and the nature of your tasks. If shorter sprints with frequent breaks work best for you, go with 30-minute blocks. If you prefer settling in for a while, experiment with 60-minute or 90-minute intervals. The goal is to find a rhythm that matches both your energy and the type of work at hand.

Reducing Decision Fatigue

Over a day, making decisions—like when to start, how long to work, or whether to take a break—can be draining. By pre-deciding block lengths and break times, you cut down on those in-the-moment calls. This consistency can be a lifesaver if you deal with issues that flare up whenever you have to choose among multiple options.

Choosing the Right Block Length

Trial and Error

There's no universal best block length. Start with something like 25 or 30 minutes and see how you feel. Were you fidgety, waiting for the timer to go off, or did you crave more time to go deeper? Did you run out of steam halfway through, or were you still raring to go when the timer ended? Based on these observations, adjust the length in small increments—five minutes longer or shorter—until you find a sweet spot. I've found, for me, when doing certain tasks a 40-minute work timer is perfect; 45 is too much and 35 isn't enough.

Consider Your Task Type

If your work demands deep concentration, such as coding or writing, you might enjoy a slightly longer block of 45 minutes to an hour. If you're handling lots of small tasks—like responding to messages, reviewing documents, or organizing files—shorter intervals might keep you from drifting. You can also mix it up: for creative or analytic tasks, use longer blocks; for administrative or routine tasks, opt for shorter ones.

Watch Out for Hyper-focus

If you tend to get lost in a task, you might think you can handle a 2- or 3-hour block. Be cautious. While hyper-focus can yield high productivity, it can also blind you to physical needs like hydration or movement. Setting a maximum block length of, say, 90 minutes can still honor your deep focus without letting you ignore your body's signals.

Planning Your Breaks

Short vs. Long Breaks

Just as block lengths vary, break lengths can too. A common pattern is 25 minutes of work followed by a 5-minute break, then every few cycles, a longer break of 15–20 minutes. If you're using longer blocks—like 45–60 minutes—you might scale your breaks to 10 or 15 minutes. Experiment with these ratios to see how well you recover between blocks. The main goal is to ensure your break is long enough to let your mind reset but not so long that you lose momentum.

What to Do During Breaks

Effective breaks aren't about scrolling on your phone until the timer dings (though sometimes a quick social media check can be okay). You might stretch, walk around, grab a glass of water, or do a brief breathing exercise. Some people find a short "brain dump" helpful—jotting down any stray thoughts that pop up during work so they don't linger. Others might take a moment to scribble notes about what they achieved in that block, setting the stage for the next one.

Avoiding the Break Trap

Neurodivergent brains might let that 5-minute break turn into 30 minutes without us noticing. Using a timer can keep breaks in check: when your short break's up, you get a nudge to return to work. If you do slip into a longer break, be compassionate with yourself, but try to identify what caused the overrun—was it a compelling YouTube video, or a lively conversation with a friend? Adjust your approach next time. Maybe a quieter break activity—like tidying your desk or making a quick snack—would be less likely to tempt you away for too long.

Setting Up a Time-Chunk Routine

Plan Your Day or Week

Decide how many blocks you want to fit into a day. Perhaps you aim for four blocks in the morning and four in the afternoon, with breaks interspersed. Leave some open space for unpredictable events or tasks that pop up. If your schedule changes day by day, it might help to make a quick plan each morning or the night before.

Assign Tasks to Each Block

Look at your to-do list and group tasks into the block that suits them. One block might go to creative work, another to administrative tasks, and so on. If you have a major project, you may dedicate several consecutive blocks, broken up by scheduled breaks. This approach is different from micro-tasking, which focuses on chopping projects into tiny steps. Here, you're slotting entire tasks or sets of tasks into a block timeframe.

Track and Adjust

Keep an eye on how well you stick to your blocks and breaks. Note whether you consistently run out of time or finish too early. Record any times you ignore the break buzzer because you're "almost done." These observations help you tweak your block lengths and break intervals. If you repeatedly find 25 minutes too short for your type of work, bump it to 30 or 35.

Reflect at the End of the Day

Take a few minutes to see which blocks went smoothly and which didn't. Did you use your breaks effectively, or did you skip them? Did you stay on task, or did you bounce around halfway through a block? Small daily reflections can lead to big improvements. Over a week or two, you'll start seeing patterns—like always being late to begin your afternoon blocks—and can make adjustments. Remember to **acknowledge your progress.**

Time Chunking Mistakes

Breaks That Vanish

Some people skip breaks, thinking they'll be more productive. In reality, the mind needs a reset. If you notice you're bulldozing through breaks, schedule them like a real appointment—no skipping allowed. Over time, you'll likely see that taking short, refreshing pauses boosts your output.

Inflexible Blocks

Life happens—meetings run long, emergencies crop up, or you simply get on a roll. If you're too rigid, you might feel stressed whenever your plan derails. One solution is to build cushion time into your schedule or be willing to shift blocks around. The goal is structure, not a straitjacket.

Task Overflow

Sometimes tasks spill beyond their assigned block, and you're left with unfinished work. If it's a recurring issue, maybe your block length is too short for that type of task. Try adding a buffer block later in the day for spillover tasks, or break the task itself into segments that fit neatly into blocks.

Perfectionism About Timing

You might feel pressure to start each block exactly on the minute, but in real life, a phone call could delay you. Don't let a small delay torpedo your entire day. Simply adjust the start time for that block and proceed. Aim for consistency, not clockwork perfection.

Maintaining a Balanced Routine

Mix Up Your Tasks

If possible, avoid filling all your morning blocks with only repetitive or draining tasks. Sprinkle in some variety. One block could be creative work, the next might be administrative, and the next for brainstorming ideas. This variety can keep your mind fresh and less prone to boredom or fatigue.

Watch Your Energy Levels

Many neurodivergent individuals find their energy peaks and dips at specific times—maybe you're razor-sharp in the morning but sluggish after lunch. Consider scheduling demanding or focus-heavy blocks during your peak energy windows. Save simpler or more routine tasks for your lower-energy times.

Pair Time Chunking with Other Strategies

Time chunking doesn't exist in a vacuum. Combine it with other methods like color-coding your to-do list or micro-tasking. For instance, in each 30-minute block, you might complete a few micro-tasks from a color-coded list. This approach lets you work on various projects without losing track of the clock.

Reviewing Your Progress

Daily or Weekly Reflection

Make it a habit to briefly assess how your time chunking went at the end of each day or week. Did you feel rushed in certain blocks? Did you skip any breaks or let them drag on too long? Jot down a note or two about what went well and what needs tweaking. Over time, you'll refine the system.

Celebrate Successful Blocks

Whenever you complete a day where you stuck to your schedule, pat yourself on the back—even if it wasn't perfect. Positive reinforcement can motivate you to keep up the practice. You might treat yourself to a favorite snack or a short walk in the evening, recognizing that you managed your day effectively. This journey is about **progress, not perfection.**

Tweak, Don't Toss

If a certain block length consistently fails, don't throw out the entire time-chunking method. Adjust it. Maybe reduce or increase the work interval by five minutes, or change the break length. The beauty of time chunking is that it's flexible. It's meant to serve you, not imprison you in a rigid system.

Mastering Manageable Slices

Chunking your time breaks that massive ocean of hours into smaller, more navigable waves. By deciding in advance how long you'll work and when you'll rest, you give your mind a sense of order.

This method is distinct from micro-tasking—rather than splitting tasks, you're structuring your work periods themselves. That difference can be huge for individuals who struggle with gauging how much time they need or maintaining momentum across a project.

For neurodivergent minds, time chunking can be a relief. It offers a consistent rhythm—work, break, work, break—making it less likely you'll wander off-track or push yourself until you're exhausted. The best part? You can tailor block lengths and break durations to your style.

Whether you're a fan of 25-minute sprints or 60-minute deep dives, the principle remains the same: *give yourself a clear window for focused work and a predictable pause to recharge.*

Over days and weeks, you'll likely notice improvements in how you approach tasks, manage energy levels, and avoid procrastination. You might even find that once-daunting projects feel more approachable, simply because you're tackling them in consistent intervals.

Go ahead—grab a timer or use a scheduling app, and chunk your time to gain control of your day. With a little trial and error, you can strike a balance that turns unstructured hours into a steady, manageable flow—leading you to a more productive, less stressful routine.

10

Digital Organization Tools

Ever felt like your tasks, notes, and random ideas live in a hundred different places—some scribbled on sticky notes, others scattered in email threads, maybe a few hidden in that dusty corner of your computer desktop? You're not alone, especially if you often juggle multiple projects or have a brain that loves hopping between ideas.

This is where digital organization tools come in. They promise a single home for your tasks, schedules, notes, and more, freeing up mental space for things you enjoy. In this chapter, we'll explore some of the most popular apps out there—like Trello and Notion—while offering tips on choosing the features that best match your personal needs.

Embrace the Lifesavers

Escaping the Scatter

Ever find yourself rummaging through different notebooks, phone apps, and email chains just to locate a single to-do item? That disjointed feeling can be particularly tough if you're prone to forgetting where you wrote something down. Going digital is a good way of consolidating everything in one spot. Instead of flipping pages or scrolling through endless messages, you open an app and—like magic—all your tasks and notes are ready for you. Less frantic searching, more time for real progress.

Updating in Real Time

Physical planners are awesome if you love handwriting. But let's face it: once you scribble something, changing it can get messy. Digital tools let you make updates instantly. If you're shifting project deadlines or rearranging priorities, you can drag tasks around or reassign them without crossing out half your to-do list (although, you can do that with sticky notes too). It's especially handy for folks who frequently change direction or get new ideas because each update is just a click or tap away.

Collaboration Without Chaos

Sometimes you need help from teammates, classmates, or family members. Rather than emailing back and forth or passing around index cards, digital apps allow everyone to see the same board, checklist, or calendar. This can cut down on miscommunication—one person changes a due date in the app, and the whole group sees it. And if you're the kind of person who gets 17 notifications every hour, it's nice to have one place to track updates instead of rummaging through chat threads.

Making Tech Work for Neurodivergent Minds

Neurodivergent people often have unique organizational needs—maybe you want colorful visuals, quick reminders, or a single platform that connects tasks to notes so you don't lose your train of thought. Digital tools can offer these features without you needing to be an expert coder. You can customize them so they match how your brain naturally works. For instance, some apps let you embed pictures, set urgent notifications, or create calming color themes so your workspace doesn't look like a neon disco.

A Quick Tour of Popular Apps

Trello: The Kanban Board Wizard

Trello is often the first app people try when they want a digital "to-do" system. It uses "boards," which act like digital bulletin boards, and "cards," which represent tasks. You can drag cards from one column to another—like moving a sticky note from "To Do" to "Done." It's visual, easy to learn, and surprisingly flexible. If you're a fan of color-coded anything, you'll enjoy Trello's labels. You can assign a hue to each card, representing urgency or categories—like "Work," "Personal," or "Must Do Before the Dog Eats My Shoes."

##Key Features of Trello

- **Drag-and-Drop Interface:** Shuffle tasks around without fuss.
- **Labels and Colors:** Keep a quick visual handle on priorities.
- **Checklists Within Cards:** Break down tasks inside each card, so you don't forget the small stuff.
- **Collaborative Boards:** Invite others, assign tasks, and see who's doing what—all on one screen.
- **Automation With Tools:** Integrate apps that allow for cards and tasks to move themselves when created/completed.

Notion: The Swiss Army Knife

If Trello is a cozy corner store, Notion is like a mega-mall: it has everything you might need under one roof—notes, tables, kanban boards, wikis, databases, calendars, you name it. That can be both a blessing and a bit intimidating if you're easily overwhelmed by too many options. But once you get the hang of it, Notion can morph into your ideal workspace, tailored exactly to your preferences. Need a page where you outline your personal goals alongside your grocery list? Or a shared board for your team's project timeline? Notion's got your back.

Key Benefits to Notion

- **All-in-One Workspace:** Mix task lists, notes, databases, and calendars on one page.
- **Templates Galore:** Start with a blank canvas or use pre-made templates for project management, budgeting, or journaling.
- **Linking and Nesting Pages:** Keep related info connected. You can embed pages within pages (like inception, but for productivity).
- **Rich Media Embeds:** Insert images, videos, or even web content to spark creativity.

Asana: Task-Focused Team Collaboration

Asana excels in a team setting, though it can also be adapted for personal use. It's more structured around tasks and sub-tasks, with deadlines and assignees visible. If you often work with groups or love seeing tasks displayed in timeline form, Asana might be your match. The interface can get busy, but if you enjoy a structured layout that lists tasks, due dates, and progress bars, it's a solid choice.

Key Features for You

- **Task Assignments and Deadlines:** Great for accountability.
- **Timeline View:** Visualize your tasks over a horizontal timeline (helpful for planning big projects).
- **Integrated Communication:** Comment directly on tasks, avoiding messy email threads.
- **Multiple Project Views:** Switch between boards, lists, or calendar formats.

Other Mention-Worthies

- **Evernote/Microsoft OneNote:** Fantastic for organizing notes, web clippings, and images.
- **Google Keep:** A minimalist approach to digital sticky notes with easy phone-to-desktop sync.
- **ClickUp:** A robust platform with features for time tracking, goals, and multiple ways to view your tasks.

Pick the Best Tool for You

Identify Your Pain Points

Before downloading every new app you see, pause and think: what's not working for you now? Are you losing track of important notes? Forgetting deadlines? Drowning in random sticky notes? List out the top two or three problems you want your digital tool to solve. If you're mainly about task management, an app like Trello or Asana might suffice. If you need deeper note-taking options, Notion or OneNote might be your jam.

Explore Key Features

Once you know your pain points, match them to app features. If you crave color-coded boards, see if the app allows it. If you want to track both tasks and notes in the same place, look for built-in note functionality or easy integration with another note-taking tool. Don't let fancy-sounding extras distract you; focus on whether the core features align with your daily workflow.

Keep It Simple

It's tempting to try everything these apps offer: Kanban boards, sub-tasks, Gantt charts, file attachments, and automation. But diving in headfirst can lead to overwhelm, especially if you're prone to giving up when things get complicated. Start with a basic setup—maybe a single board in Trello or a single page in Notion. Gradually add layers if you find you truly need them. This slow approach helps you avoid the pitfall of turning your digital workspace into a labyrinth.

Test, Then Commit

Try an app for a week or two. If it feels clunky, no harm done—migrate your tasks to another platform. Most apps have free tiers, so you're not locked into a subscription unless you upgrade. Once you settle on a tool that clicks, invest time in learning it well. Watch a few tutorials or explore user guides so you can make the most of the features that matter to you.

Avoiding Digital Overload

The All-Too-Common Trap

Digital organization is supposed to simplify life, but it can turn into digital clutter if you're not careful. Some people end up with multiple apps—one for tasks, one for notes, another for budgeting—and lose track of which detail lives where. If you're prone to confusion or find novelty irresistible, you might keep bouncing from one platform to the next, never fully settling. This can be as chaotic as having sticky notes plastered everywhere.

Consolidate Where Possible

If you choose Notion, for instance, consider using it for notes, tasks, and project outlines so you're not scattering info across four different apps. You can still keep simpler tools for specialized needs (like a budget spreadsheet in Google Sheets) but aim to limit the number of places you store essential data. The more consolidated your system, the fewer "Where did I put that?" moments you'll face.

Set Review Periods

To keep your digital tool from becoming a graveyard of abandoned tasks, schedule a weekly or monthly check-in. Review what's in the app, clear out old or done items, and tidy up the layout. This small habit can prevent the dreaded digital junk pile, where half your tasks belong in the trash and the other half are outdated.

Integrations and Automation

Linking Tools Together

Most modern digital organization apps talk to each other—or at least they can if you set them up. You might link your calendar to Trello, so due dates appear in both places. Or sync Notion with Google Drive if you store images and documents there. Integrations can save time, but only if they genuinely solve a need. Be cautious: hooking up too many tools can lead to complexity that cancels out any gains.

Automating Routine Tasks

Some apps let you set up "if this, then that" triggers. For example, if you add a new card in Trello for a client project, an integration might automatically create a matching folder in your cloud drive. While these automations can be cool, they also require careful setup. If your brain goes numb at the mention of "webhooks," skip the advanced stuff and stick to basic features that you'll use regularly.

Digital Dilemmas

Shiny App Syndrome

You hear about a new, revolutionary organization tool every other week, and you're tempted to switch immediately. Constantly jumping from one platform to another can waste time and energy. Give each new tool a fair test. If it doesn't solve problems better than your current system, stick to what you have.

Over-Organizing

You know that feeling when you decide to "get organized" and suddenly you're creating color-coded sections for your color-coded sections? Maybe you've spent two hours categorizing tasks, only to realize you haven't done any of them. Sometimes, we get so excited about setting up a system that we forget the system exists to help us get stuff done.

Keep categories broad enough that you can glance at your layout and know what's going on. The goal isn't to become the best digital tool user in the galaxy—it's to free your mind from the stress of juggling tasks manually.

Forgetting to Update

Even the best digital tool won't help if you never input new tasks or mark items as done. Make it a habit. Each morning or evening, spend a few minutes logging updates. Over time, this check-in can become as automatic as brushing your teeth.

Ignoring Mobile vs. Desktop

Some apps excel on mobile but are clunky on desktop, or vice versa. If you're always on the go, a robust mobile app might be essential. Test each platform on both your phone and computer. If one version is terrible, consider whether that's a deal-breaker.

No Backup Plan

Digital tools can fail, or you might lose internet access at a critical moment. Keep critical info in a second safe place, or at least export your tasks or notes regularly. Many apps have built-in backups or let you export data. This ensures you're not left high and dry if a server goes down or you accidentally delete something important.

Personalize Your Workspace

Theme and Layout

Some apps let you change background images, colors, or fonts. If a gentle pastel tone or a serene beach photo helps you stay calm, go for it. Personalizing your workspace can make you more inclined to open the app regularly, especially if you're the type who loves a dash of aesthetic appeal.

Dashboards

Tools like Notion offer "dashboard" pages that serve as your homepage. You might include a calendar widget, a section for daily tasks, and a quick link to your notes. It's like having a personalized control panel for your life. Just be sure not to clutter it with so many widgets that it slows you down.

Accessibility Features

If you need specific accessibility options—like high-contrast themes, screen readers, or keyboard shortcuts—check if the app supports them. This can be a make-or-break factor, especially if you rely on assistive technology. Don't assume every shiny new app meets these needs; do a quick check or test drive first.

Tips for Long-Term Success

Start Small, Grow Steadily

Launch with the bare minimum setup—maybe a board for your personal life in Trello or a single workspace in Notion. Once you're confident with the basics, try adding a second board or a new type of page. This keeps the learning curve gentle and helps you avoid turning your system into an unmanageable monster overnight.

Pair with Real-Life Routines

If you naturally review your day over morning coffee, open your app right then to check your plan. If you typically wind down at night by clearing out emails, take a quick peek at your digital tool to see what's on deck for tomorrow. Attaching the app to an existing daily habit can help it become second nature.

Periodic Clean-Up

Every few weeks, scan your digital setup. Do you still need that backlog of random tasks from two months ago? Are there notes or pages you haven't touched in ages? Archive or delete what's outdated. This not only keeps the interface clean but also prevents you from feeling like you're sifting through digital junk.

Don't Obsess Over Perfection

It's okay if your system isn't picture-perfect. Some people post glamorous screenshots of their meticulously designed Notion pages or color-coded Trello boards, which can set unrealistic standards. The real question is whether your system helps you accomplish tasks and stay less stressed, not whether it looks Instagram-worthy.

Harnessing Digital Tools Without Drowning

Digital organization tools can be your best ally if you often feel scattered, forgetful, or overloaded. They gather your tasks, ideas, and resources in one place, making it easier to manage the details of everyday life. From Trello's friendly drag-and-drop boards to Notion's all-in-one versatility, there's likely an app that fits your style.

Just remember to approach these tools with clear goals in mind. Which problem(s) are you trying to solve? Which features make your life simpler? Stay watchful for the pitfalls—like diving into too many apps or over-organizing until you need a map to find your to-do list.

With a bit of self-awareness and a willingness to experiment, you can end up with a digital system that's less "digital clutter" and more "digital clarity." And hey, if you ever catch yourself color-coding color codes, take a breath and remember: **the point is to get things done,** *not to create an award-winning digital museum exhibit.* In the end, a system that helps you find your tasks quickly and keeps you sane is the real gold medal.

11

Visual Timers

Have you ever stared at a countdown clock during a sports game, feeling the tension rise as the seconds tick away? There's something about seeing time pass in a visual way that nudges us into action—or at least captures our attention.

For many people, especially those with neurodivergent minds, the idea of "time" can be slippery. One hour might race by in a blink, while ten minutes can drag on like an eternity. Visual timers offer a simple fix: they make time visible.

Instead of trying to hold a vague notion of "fifteen minutes left" in your head, you see it shrink before your eyes, and that changes how you work. This chapter takes a look at why visual timers can be so powerful, how to choose one that fits your style, and practical tips for using them day-to-day.

Why Seeing Time Matters

The Brain's Need for Tangibility

Many of us can grasp physical objects easily. We know how heavy a book feels in our hands or how big a plate of food looks on the table. Time, on the other hand, is invisible—until it's too late and we're racing to meet a deadline. This intangible nature of time often frustrates people who struggle with planning or transitions. A visual timer brings that invisibility to light, giving you something you can watch as it moves.

Imagine a simple hourglass: each grain of sand trickling from top to bottom shows time melting away. It's oddly satisfying (or maybe nerve-wracking, depending on your mood) to see the supply of sand shrink. That direct visual feedback can snap us out of daydreaming or procrastination. It's like your mind says, "Oh, look, the timer's halfway through—I should keep going." Instead of a fleeting sense of "I must hurry," you see a real, physical process that pushes you forward.

Urgency Without Panic

Deadlines can cause stress—who hasn't felt their heart race at the thought of finishing a task "by 5:00 p.m."? But if you rely only on numbers in your head or on a clock, you might not register how quickly 5:00 p.m. is approaching until it's nearly upon you.

A visual timer, whether a gadget or an on-screen bar, subtly injects urgency into your routine without sending you into a full-blown panic. Rather than that last-second scramble, you get small reminders every time your eyes flick to the timer. The gentle nudge can help you pace yourself, aiming for a smooth finish rather than a mad rush.

A Tool for Mindful Transitions

Transitions—like switching from one task to another—can be tough, especially if you're hyper-focused or anxious about change. Knowing you have three minutes left on a visible timer can soften the jump. You can use those minutes to mentally wrap up your current task, jot down quick notes for where to pick up next time and prepare your brain for the next activity. It's much easier to manage transitions when you see them coming.

Timer Styles to Consider

Classic Countdown Timers

Think of those small digital devices you might find in a kitchen drawer. You set a number—say 20 minutes—and it counts down to zero, often beeping when time's up. While these are common, many of them only show numbers. If you want a purely numeric display, this might be fine. But if you're looking for a more visual representation, you might explore timers that highlight the passage of time in a more dynamic way (like changing colors or showing a shrinking pie chart).

- **Best For:** People who don't need constant visual feedback but just want a beep or alarm when time's up.
- **Drawback:** You won't necessarily see how much time remains unless you pick up the device and check it.

Analog Disk Timers

You've likely seen a timer with a colored disk that disappears as time goes on. For instance, you twist the dial to set 30 minutes, and a red section fills the face of the timer. As the timer counts down, the red portion shrinks. This style can be a game-changer for those who want a silent, continuous visual. Without needing to read numbers, you can glance over and see that half the color is gone, meaning you're halfway through your block.

- **Best For:** Glances and constant visual updates.
- **Drawback:** Typically mechanical, so it might tick or make noise. Some find the ticking reassuring; others find it irritating.

Hourglass and Sand Timers

It's the oldest method in the book—literally centuries old. You flip the hourglass and watch the sand move from top to bottom. Today, you can find hourglasses with different durations, from 1 minute to a full hour. They're visually appealing and can be a neat desk accessory.

- **Best For:** A simple, tactile way to see time slip by.
- **Drawback:** You can't pause or easily measure partial intervals. You have to flip it at the end to restart.

App-Based Visual Timers

Plenty of apps and websites now show time passing in visually striking ways: color blocks shrinking, circles spinning, or progress bars filling up. Some feature calming animations, while others go for bright, intense visuals. You can pick an app that resonates with you, from minimalist designs with a single color to quirky ones featuring cartoon characters or scenic backgrounds.

- **Best For:** People who are near their computer or phone and prefer digital alerts and customizable visuals.
- **Drawback:** It's easy to get distracted by notifications or windows if you're on a device.

Wearable Timers

This category is the newest of the bunch. Some fitness trackers or smart-watches can display countdowns on your wrist or buzz when time's up. A few specialized wearables even show tiny progress bars or colors. This can help if you need a discreet timer during a meeting or class. You glance at your wrist, notice time slipping away, and stay on track without pulling out a phone or device.

- **Best For:** Subtle reminders and on-the-go tasks.
- **Drawback:** Small screen sizes might not be super visible, and you might end up distracted by other smartwatch features.

Setting Up Your Visual Timer Routine

Picking the Right Duration

Before you pick which style of timer to use, consider how you'll chunk your time. If you're typically working on a short task—like a 5-minute tidying blitz—you might go with something quick and obvious, like an analog disk timer set to 5 minutes. If you're usually working on a longer project—maybe 45 minutes of solid focus—an app-based timer with a calm, color-changing progress bar might be more your style.

The key is matching the timer's length to the nature of your task. Using a 30-minute timer for a 5-minute chore can feel like overkill, and the mismatch might lead you to ignore the timer altogether.

Positioning for Easy Glances

A visual timer only helps if you can see it without interrupting your flow. If you're using a physical device, put it on your desk where you can spot it with peripheral vision. For an app, maybe keep it open in a small window or pinned tab. Adjust brightness or color settings so it's noticeable but not distracting. You don't want to end up hypnotized by the swirling circle, forgetting the actual work you set out to do.

Pairing with Breaks

Visual timers can also mark when it's time to take a break. If you've decided on a 25-minute work block, set the timer. Once you see that color disk vanish or the bar reaches zero, stop. This is especially helpful if you're someone who either forgets to pause or hyper-focuses until your body protests *(Hi there, it's me!*). Knowing that a short rest is coming might nudge you to push through a tough moment, or it might remind you that your body and mind need a breather.

Encouraging Task Transitions

Let's say you struggle with shifting from one activity to another. You can set a timer to transition gracefully. For instance, if you plan to switch from writing an email to preparing lunch, you might run a 10-minute timer for "wrap-up." When that timer runs out, you've ideally closed your email tab, noted any pending tasks, and mentally prepped for the next activity. The visual aspect of that timer can keep you mindful about not drifting into an extra 20 minutes of random internet browsing.

Overcoming Common Timer Hurdles

Timer Anxiety

Some people feel anxious watching time slip away—like an exam countdown that triggers panic. If that's you, consider using a more neutral visual timer. Maybe pick calm colors or an app that frames the passage of time in a gentler way, like a fading pastel bar instead of a loud siren-like countdown. Also, remind yourself the timer is a helper, not a drill sergeant. You can always reset or pause if you truly need more time.

Ignoring the Timer

We've all had that moment where the buzzer goes off, and we think, "Meh, I'm good to just keep going." If this becomes a habit, the timer loses its power. One trick is to build a small consequence for ignoring it. For example, tell yourself you can't *[insert reward here]* until you properly reset or acknowledge the timer. Another approach is to physically move the timer out of reach so you can't just hit snooze without thinking. That extra effort might nudge you to respect its authority.

Overuse Leading to Stress

Visual timers are great, but having them run all day, every day can turn life into a series of countdowns that feel relentless. If you notice stress creeping in—like you're perpetually racing a clock—step back. You don't need a timer for every second. Use it strategically for tasks where time slipping away is a known problem. For other parts of your day, let yourself breathe without the ticking clock in sight.

Wrong Timer for the Task

Not every timer fits every situation. If you're painting a landscape and want to remain in a creative zone, a loud ticking analog disk might disrupt your rhythm. In that case, a subtle, color-changing app in the corner of your screen might be better. Match your timer style to the environment and the nature of the task.

Small, Practical Tips for Success

- **Label Your Blocks:** If you're using an app-based timer, you can name each session (e.g., "Write Blog Post" or "Plan Dinner"). That way, when you see the countdown, you recall why you set it in the first place. *(**Pro tip:** if you're using a digital system like Trello, some apps will set the timer for you based on your cards.)*
- **Consider Sound Settings:** A jarring alarm can be effective but also stressful. Experiment with gentle chimes or even bird sounds. If you're the type who's immune to soft alerts, go ahead and pick a louder ring—just don't scare the wildlife.
- **Use Colors Wisely:** If your timer has color options, choose hues that help your concentration. Maybe a soothing blue helps you stay calm, while a bright red might keep you alert. Avoid neon blinking if you're easily

overstimulated.
- **Share Timers with Others:** If you have a roommate, friend, or family member who also struggles with time, you can set a shared timer for group tasks or chores. Seeing the same countdown can foster teamwork: "We have 15 minutes left to tidy the living room—let's do it!"
- **Track Patterns Over Time:** Some digital timers log your sessions, showing how many times you used them or how consistent you were. If you like data, reviewing these logs can offer insights—like noticing you're more productive in the morning or that 20-minute sessions work better than 40-minute ones.

Combining with Other Strategies

Visual timers can mesh nicely with other techniques—like body doubling, micro-tasks, or chunking your time (as mentioned in earlier chapters). You might run a 15-minute timer for a micro-task block or use it alongside color-coded to-do lists. The point is synergy, not duplication.

Timer Challenges

Becoming Timer-Dependent

Relying on a timer for every single thing can backfire; you might lose the ability to gauge time without it. Aim for balance—use it when it's helpful, but also practice internal time estimation for smaller tasks.

Ignoring Time Cues

If you keep setting the timer and ignoring it when zero hits, it's no better than having no timer at all. Decide in advance how you'll respond when it rings or the color runs out.

Too Loud, Too Distracting

An over-the-top timer might make you anxious or annoyed. If you cringe every time it ticks, find a gentler version. The goal is to help, not stress you out.

Picking the Wrong Format

A phone app with cartoon animations might be fun, but if you hate phone notifications, you'll probably ignore it. If you detest mechanical ticking, don't pick an analog device. Test different formats until something feels right.

A Clear Look at Time

When time remains hidden in the back of our minds, it's easy to lose track. Visual timers put it front and center, giving you a gentle push to stay on task or switch gears. For many neurodivergent individuals, this clarity can be transformative—suddenly, tasks that feel endless have a defined window, and transitions feel less abrupt.

Visual timers can be the friendliest alarm clock you've ever met—showing you how much time you've got left without shouting at you (usually). If you ever feel the urge to roll your eyes at it, remember: you're the boss. The timer is just your assistant. If it starts feeling like your boss, give it a silly name or a funny face sticker. A small joke like that can defuse the tension of watching the countdown.

You set the frame, you decide the length, and you watch it unfold in real time. Whether it's a bright-red dial shrinking on your desk or a color-changing bar on your computer screen, that visual anchor can guide your day in a calmer, more intentional way.

Just remember not to let the timer run your life. It's a tool, not a tyrant. Start by testing one for a small task, see how it feels, and adapt as you go. Maybe you'll become a devout fan of those red disk timers or discover an app that's your perfect match.

With a bit of experimentation, you'll find a way to make time visible in a way that suits your rhythm—keeping you grounded, motivated, and more in control of your schedule than ever before.

12

Mind Mapping

The human brain is a bustling city of ideas, thoughts, and images flying in every direction. Sometimes they move so quickly that it's hard to track where one thought ends and another begins. Enter mind mapping: a visual technique that helps you capture the chaos and place it in a clear, easy-to-follow diagram.

Instead of wrestling with long lists or dense paragraphs, you turn your thoughts into bubbles, branches, and connectors, painting a vivid picture of what you're thinking. This style of note-taking and planning can be a huge help if you're neurodivergent—or simply someone who thinks better in pictures than in lines of text.

In this chapter, we'll explore how mind mapping can tame scattered ideas, offer fresh angles on problems, and keep your projects on track without drowning in mental clutter.

Why Mind Mapping?

Making the Abstract Concrete

Have you ever tried explaining a complex idea in words, only to feel like it's slipping through your fingers? That's because some concepts don't behave like neat lists. They branch out and interconnect, forming a web of related points. Mind maps let you lay out each of those points visually.

Instead of writing "Point A leads to Point B" in a sentence, you draw a line between two bubbles. This structure mirrors the brain's associative thinking—where one idea triggers another, which in turn sparks a different connection.

Breaking the Line-by-Line Habit

Traditional outlines can be restrictive, especially for neurodivergent brains which can jump like an electron from one atom to the other going from one idea to the next in rapid-fire bursts. With a mind map, you're free to place ideas wherever they naturally seem to belong, and then draw connections later.

You might start in the center with a main topic, then branch out in several directions at once—like a tree's limbs growing from the trunk. This non-linear approach suits people who find straight lists or bullet points too confining.

Engaging Both Sides of the Brain

Although the "left brain vs. right brain" idea is more metaphorical than literal, there is truth to the fact that creativity and logic often mix in surprising ways. Mind mapping can stimulate both. You have the creative freedom to doodle, use colors, or add quirky symbols, but you also bring order as you decide how branches connect. This blend can be especially helpful if you have a mind that jumps between big-picture creativity and nitty-gritty details faster than a caffeinated hummingbird.

The Basics of a Mind Map

Central Idea

The heart of any mind map is the main concept, question, or topic you're exploring. Write or draw it in the center of the page. Many mind mappers like to circle or highlight this central bubble to set it apart. If you're a visual thinker, you could even replace text with a small sketch of the idea. For instance, if your central topic is "Vacation Planning," you might draw a small suitcase or palm tree.

Branches and Sub-Branches

From that central node, you'll draw branches outward, each labeled with a sub-topic or related idea. These branches can then sprout their own smaller branches if you need to break things down further. Think of it like a tree: the trunk is your core topic, the big branches are your main themes, and each twig is a specific detail. This nested structure keeps your ideas visually grouped while preserving a sense of hierarchy—so you know which points belong under which category.

Symbols, Colors, and Doodles

One of the joys of mind mapping is how flexible it can be. You can use colored pens, highlight certain branches, or add tiny icons to indicate urgency or importance. A small exclamation point might mark an especially critical sub-idea, while a light-bulb doodle could signal a fresh insight. By sprinkling in a bit of color or imagery, you make the map more engaging and memorable. For some neurodivergent minds, these playful elements can also reduce the feeling that you're "just doing work," making the process more inviting.

Lines and Connectors

Ideas rarely exist in a vacuum—often one sub-point relates to another sub-point on a different branch. In a linear document, you might say, "See Section 2.4" or create a footnote. In a mind map, you can draw a line from one bubble to another, visually showing the link. This immediate, tangible representation of connections can be a huge "aha" moment, revealing relationships you hadn't noticed before.

How Mind Mapping Helps Neurodivergent Thinkers

Embracing Associative Thinking

People with ADHD, autism, dyslexia, or other neurodivergent traits often describe their minds as "busy," "non-linear," or "constantly jumping." A mind map meets that style head-on. Instead of forcing thoughts into tidy paragraphs, you sketch them as a web of linked nodes. If your brain leaps from one idea to a seemingly unrelated one, you can just add a new branch. Over time, you might see patterns forming, or realize how those "unrelated" thoughts connect.

Visual Over Verbal

For some individuals, words on a page can blur together or feel restrictive. Seeing everything laid out in shapes and colors might be more intuitive. That sense of "I get it now" can come quicker when ideas are physically spaced out instead of crammed into a single block of text. Mind maps also let you skim for crucial points by scanning for visual cues—like which bubble is largest or which has a star drawn on it.

Alternative Thinking

Long to-do lists or giant project outlines can be overwhelming, especially if you're grappling with executive functioning challenges. Mind mapping offers a gentler, more creative route. Instead of a rigid list that screams, "Look how many items you have to do," the map spreads tasks out in a more organic way. You can tackle them one branch at a time, focusing on whichever cluster feels most important. The bright colors and minimal text can make the workload seem more approachable.

Freedom to Brainstorm Wildly

Those in the neurodivergent spectrum sometimes hold back in brainstorming sessions, worried they might propose ideas that are "too random." A mind map invites random ideas. Place them in their mini-bubble, connect them if you see a link, or let them float. **No idea seems too outlandish when everything else is forming a network of possibilities.**

Building Clear Mind Maps

Keep It Centered

Always place your main topic in the middle. That way, your eyes naturally move outward in all directions. If you start in the corner or on one side, you might unconsciously limit how far you extend branches. The center-based layout is what makes mind maps both visually balanced and mentally freeing.

Limit Text in Each Bubble

A mind map is about capturing concepts, not writing mini-essays in each node. If you find yourself typing entire paragraphs, consider creating a separate note or document for detailed explanations. In the bubble, stick to a keyword or a brief phrase—enough to jog your memory or convey the essence. This practice keeps your map airy and digestible.

Use Hierarchy Wisely

You don't want one branch to sprawl into untold levels of detail, especially if it's overshadowing the rest of the map. Group smaller points together or create a separate offshoot if one branch gets too dense. Some mind mappers use thicker lines for major branches and thinner lines for sub-branches, giving a quick visual cue about each point's importance.

Mind the Clutter

Ironically, mind maps can become chaotic if you over-stuff them with doodles, colors, and connections. Aim for a balance—use images and colors to highlight key ideas, but keep plenty of white space. If one area feels overloaded, consider starting a secondary mind map just for that sub-topic. Remember, the goal is clarity, not creating a vibrant collage that's impossible to read.

Apply Consistent Styling

Pick a color scheme or font style and stick to it across the map. Maybe you use one color for headings, another for sub-points, and a third for notes. That consistency reduces mental overhead, so your brain knows, "Pink boxes are new ideas, and green boxes are final decisions." A quick look will reveal the nature of each branch without deciphering a brand-new design each time.

Practical Uses of Mind Mapping

Project Planning

Whether you're organizing a community event or developing a product, mind maps can help identify tasks, deadlines, and resources. You could have a main bubble labeled "Event Plan," with branches for "Venue," "Budget," "Marketing," and "Volunteers." Each branch then sprouts further details. This visual approach can keep you from forgetting vital steps—like checking for permits or printing fliers.

Study Notes

Students (of all ages) often find mind maps helpful for summarizing chapters or lectures. Instead of re-reading multiple pages of text, you convert the information into a single sheet of connected ideas. Later, you can glance at your map to recall the main points. The act of creating the map also cements the knowledge in your mind—far more than passively reading or highlighting might.

Brainstorming New Ideas

Staring at a blank page can be intimidating, but a mind map template encourages you to toss out words, images, or mini-ideas without judgment. You can scribble ideas on different branches, connect them if they spark new insights, and build out from there. This method can help generate solutions for problems or fresh concepts for creative projects.

Decision-Making

Mind maps aren't just for capturing info; they can also help you weigh options. Suppose you're deciding between a few career paths. You might place "Career Choice" in the center and have branches for each option. Under each branch, you list pros, cons, potential salaries, or required qualifications. Seeing everything laid out visually makes comparisons more intuitive.

Personal Reflection

Some like to use mind mapping as a journaling tool. You might place "Personal Growth" in the center and create branches for "Strengths," "Goals," "Challenges," and "Habits." By fleshing out each branch, you get a holistic view of where you stand and where you want to improve. The result could be an honest snapshot of your life at that moment.

Mind Mapping Tools

Pen and Paper

The simplest approach requires zero tech: a blank sheet and some colored pens or pencils. Many people enjoy the tactile, flexible nature of physically drawing lines and doodles. You can also use sticky notes if you want to rearrange ideas without erasing them. Paper mind maps are great for quick sketches, and they can feel more personal, but they're harder to edit if your ideas shift dramatically.

Whiteboards

If you love standing and moving around while you think, a whiteboard might be your canvas. This can be helpful in team settings, too—colleagues gather around, toss out ideas, and watch the map grow in real-time. Just make sure to take a photo or transcribe it before someone accidentally erases everything.

Digital Apps

Numerous apps and programs focus on mind mapping, letting you create, expand, and reorganize with simple clicks. Some popular ones include MindMeister, XMind, and Coggle. Many have drag-and-drop interfaces, color-coding, and the ability to attach links or files to each node. The advantage is easy editing and sharing. However, watch for feature overload—

some apps bury basic mind mapping under too many bells and whistles.

Staying Motivated to Use Mind Maps

Start Small

Don't aim to create an elaborate, museum-worthy map on your first try. Pick a simple topic—like "Groceries for This Week"—and practice branching out. The point is to get used to visual thinking, not to produce a work of art. As you grow comfortable, you can try mind-mapping bigger projects or deeper reflections.

Keep It Accessible

Hang your paper map somewhere visible, or pin a screenshot of your digital map to your desktop. If your mind map stays hidden in a folder, you'll forget to update it. Seeing it daily can spark new ideas or remind you of tasks you haven't tackled yet. If you're worried about it becoming cluttered, schedule a quick review or clean-up session every few days.

Combine with Other Methods (Selectively)

While you don't want to weigh yourself down with too many systems, you can pair mind mapping with simpler tools. For example, if your mind map reveals 10 tasks you must do, you might transfer those tasks to a to-do list or digital planner. The mind map stays your big-picture guide, while the to-do list handles day-to-day execution. This can be especially handy if you prefer quick checklists for daily tasks but still want the creative freedom of a mind map for brainstorming.

Involve Others

Sharing a mind map can be an adventure. In a study group or work team, each person can add their ideas or links, creating a shared "thought bubble." Just be prepared for the map to grow in unexpected directions. Sometimes collaboration sparks brilliant innovations; other times it reveals that your coworker's sense of humor revolves around turning every bubble into a pun. Either way, it's a unique way to see how different minds approach the same topic.

Don't Get Lost in the Maze

Over-stuffing the Map

You might try to cram everything you know into one page. If it starts looking like a Jackson Pollock painting, step back. Break it into multiple smaller maps or create sub-maps for complex sections.

Lack of Focus

If your central topic isn't clearly defined, your branches will meander without direction. Make sure you have a solid, concise main idea before branching out.

Forgetting Hierarchy

Keep track of what's a main branch and what's a sub-branch. Mixing up the levels can make the map confusing to review. Use slightly different colors, fonts, or bubble shapes to mark key points vs. minor details.

Neglecting to Revisit

A mind map is a living document, meant to evolve as your project or thinking progresses. If you treat it like a one-time doodle and never look at it again, it'll lose its usefulness. Schedule check-ins if the map is for an ongoing project.

Obsessing Over Visuals

Yes, it's fun to add doodles and color-code each branch, but if you spend an hour perfecting the lettering on one bubble, you're missing the point. Aim for clarity and usefulness, not museum-ready art.

Mapping It Up

Mind mapping transforms intangible thoughts into a living blueprint on the page or screen. By focusing on a central idea and radiating outwards, you capture not just the "what" but also the "why" and "how" behind each sub-point.

For neurodivergent minds that crave freedom from rigid formats, it's a chance to let ideas breathe and connect in a way that feels natural. Remember, mind maps are as flexible as you make them. If you prefer bright colors and doodles, go for it. If a minimalist black-and-white scheme keeps your mind at ease, that's fine too.

The method's core strength is how it welcomes spontaneity and structure in one place. Feel free to create multiple branches, link them in surprising ways, and see your big ideas evolve. As you become more comfortable with mind mapping, you might notice it popping up in everyday scenarios—planning parties, troubleshooting issues at work, or even sorting through personal goals.

Whenever you sense your thoughts scattering in all directions, step back, sketch a center bubble, and let the branches flow. You'll find clarity hiding right there in the lines and shapes, ready to help you make sense of your next step.

III

Routines and Accountability

"Motivation gets you started, but habits keep you going."

Routines and accountability are the unsung heroes of productivity—quiet, dependable forces that shape the flow of our days and steer us toward our goals. This section dives into the art of building routines that stick and systems that hold you steady.

These chapters will show you how to make structure work for you. It's time to trade the chaos of constant course corrections for the calm clarity of a plan that adapts as you do.

13

Flexible Schedules

The morning sun streamed through the window, casting a warm glow on your workspace. Coffee steaming, you were in the zone, checking off to-dos like a machine. Then, buzz, your phone lit up. "School closed due to a burst water pipe. Kids go home early." Suddenly, that perfectly arranged schedule was crumpled faster than a paper airplane.Sound familiar?

We've all been there. Rigid plans are brittle; they shatter at the first sign of disruption. A flexible schedule, however, is like a willow tree in the wind – it bends, it adapts, it doesn't break. Think of it as having extra time cushions built-in, ready to absorb those everyday shocks. So how do we create a schedule that's both structured and adaptable?

Why Flexible Schedules Matter

Stress Management

A jam-packed calendar might look impressive—every minute accounted for, from sunrise to bedtime. But the downside is it leaves you zero breathing space. The moment something goes off-script, you're forced to rearrange everything, often spiraling into stress or guilt because you can't keep up. With a bit of buffer time, you can absorb minor delays or last-minute needs without feeling like the whole day collapses. This approach proves especially valuable if you're the kind of person who tends to internalize stress or quickly feels overwhelmed by changes.

Self-Trust and Adaptability

When you plan with more fluid blocks of time instead of rock-solid appointments, you send yourself a subtle message: "I trust myself to handle it." Instead of needing external constraints—like a rigid alarm for every single task—you rely on your sense of timing and priorities. You learn to adapt moment by moment, building resilience. If you're neurodivergent, or simply prone to creative thinking, this can feel like a more natural way to organize your day. You aren't pinned down by an unchangeable timeline, so your schedule can flow with your energy levels and fresh ideas.

Mental Space for Creativity

Rigid schedules can choke spontaneity. You might pass up a spark of inspiration because your calendar says you should be returning emails right now. With flexible scheduling, if you feel a surge of creative energy for writing, painting, or brainstorming, you can roll with it. Knowing that you've built in time cushions, you're free to follow these moments of inspiration. This balance between structure and spontaneity often leads to more fulfilling—and surprising—results.

Elements of a Flexible Schedule

Core Anchors

First, identify the few activities or commitments in your day that can't be shifted, like an online meeting or a doctor's appointment. These become your anchors. If they're time-sensitive, block them out as they are. Then you can build the rest of the schedule around these immovable spots. Anchors might also be personal habits, like a daily workout, prayer time, or a dinner routine with family. By keeping these anchors in place, you ensure you don't lose track of what truly matters or what's non-negotiable.

Buffer Blocks

Between these anchors, insert "buffer blocks" of flexible time. For example, say you have an important meeting from 9:00 to 10:00 a.m., and then a lunch date at 12:30 p.m. You could schedule a buffer block from 10:00 to 12:00. That two-hour window is for tasks you need to handle, but you don't specify every five-minute increment in advance. If something takes longer than expected, you can adjust. If you finish early, you might use the leftover time for personal errands or maybe reading that book you've been meaning to start.

Soft Deadlines

A flexible schedule doesn't mean ignoring deadlines altogether. Instead, you can set "soft deadlines"—loose targets for when to have certain tasks done, acknowledging that life happens. For instance, you might decide to wrap up a report by the end of the week, with a personal goal of finishing by Thursday so you have a day's buffer. If it's done on Thursday, great! If not, you have Friday to polish it without panicking. This approach reduces last-minute chaos because you've given yourself a fallback.

Task Clusters

Rather than scheduling each to-do item at a specific time, you group similar tasks into "clusters." Maybe you have a cluster for email and messaging in the morning, a cluster for creative work after lunch, and a cluster for errands in the late afternoon. As long as you handle those tasks during their clusters, you're good. There's no need to say, "At 1:05 p.m., I must start writing." You just know that after lunch, you'll focus on writing for a while, and if something urgent interrupts, you'll still have some wiggle room to shift things around.

Flexible Routines

Routines provide the skeleton of your day, but you can keep them soft. For example, you might aim to wake up at around 7:00 a.m., do some light exercise, and then check emails. But if you woke up feeling groggy or you got to bed later, you might shift that exercise block by an hour or shorten the email session. The routine is there to guide you, but it's not set in stone.

Wiggle Room With Structure

Set Minimum and Maximum Times

One trick is to assign both a minimum and a maximum duration for certain activities. For example, decide that you'll spend at least 15 minutes on a creative project each afternoon, but no more than 45 minutes unless you're really in the zone. This ensures you're not skipping the activity entirely, but also not letting it dominate your day if something else demands attention.

Plan for Interruptions

We all know interruptions happen—phone calls, knocks on the door, kids needing help, or a random chore popping up. Instead of letting them ruin your day, factor them in. Perhaps you block out 20–30 minutes during each half of the day as a "catch-up" period. If an interruption occurs, you use that catch-up slot to finish whatever got delayed. If no interruptions happen (lucky you!), you can treat that time as a bonus break or get ahead on something else.

Overlapping or Floating Time Blocks

If you manage multiple projects, consider floating blocks of time that can be applied to any of them. For instance, you might schedule a "Project Work" window from 2:00 to 4:00 p.m. but let yourself decide that day which project you'll tackle. This way, your schedule remains structured (work happens from 2:00 to 4:00), yet flexible (which project you choose is open). It keeps you from feeling boxed in while still maintaining a routine of focused effort.

Align with Energy Levels

Many neurodivergent people find their energy or attention spikes at odd hours or dips unpredictably. If possible, place the tasks needing the most concentration or creativity in your known high-energy periods. The times when you're usually low on energy can serve as a buffer for simpler tasks or errands. Of course, real life might not always accommodate this, but even small adjustments—like shifting intense work a half-hour earlier—can pay off.

Dodge the Delays

Endless Procrastination

With so much flexibility, you risk pushing tasks off indefinitely. If you're prone to procrastination, try placing those "soft deadlines" or anchoring tasks at some point in the day. You could say, "By 4:00 p.m., I want these three emails sent," or "I'll start that reading no later than 8:00 p.m." Gentle lines in the sand can keep your day from melting into an ocean of undone tasks.

Lack of Clarity

Too much flexibility can leave you unsure of what you're supposed to be doing at any given moment. If you find yourself floundering, a simple fix is to set a smaller number of buffer blocks. Instead of having one giant open chunk for the entire afternoon, break it into two or three mini-blocks, each for a specific category of tasks (e.g., "Work," "Household Chores," "Personal Projects").

Missing Hard Commitments

Some tasks genuinely need specific times—like picking up a child from school or hosting a live Zoom session. Make sure you don't bury those "hard" commitments under the flexibility. Keep them marked, maybe with a bright color in your calendar or phone reminder. If your day is too fluid, you risk forgetting about these immovable anchors altogether.

Over-scheduling Buffer Time

Oddly enough, you can have too many buffers, leading to a day that feels so open you never get into a productive groove. If your schedule is 90% slack, you may wander aimlessly. The key is to find that sweet spot—enough slack to handle the unexpected, but not so much that you're swimming in free-floating hours.

Tools for Flexible Planning

Paper Calendars with Pencil

Yes, old-school works. If you prefer a paper planner or bullet journal, write down your anchors in pen so they stand out, but pencil in your buffer blocks or to-do clusters. If something changes, you can erase or rewrite without feeling you messed up the entire page.

Digital Calendars

Most calendar apps let you drag and drop events, making them easy to shift if new plans arise. Consider color-coding your events: one color for anchors (the "must-do" items) and a softer hue for flexible blocks. Some apps even allow for "tentative" time slots that show up differently from confirmed events, signaling that they're open for reconfiguration.

Task Management Apps

If you'd rather keep tasks separate from a time-based layout, use a digital to-do list where you group tasks by day or by category, but don't assign each one a strict time. As the day unfolds, you decide which cluster to handle, and in what order, within the day's available windows. This method often pairs well with a basic calendar that only holds anchors.

Timers and Reminders

If you worry about losing track of time in your buffer blocks, set gentle reminders. You could have an alarm that nudges you at the end of each block to check if you need to move on. Keep the alerts low-key—maybe a soft chime or vibration—so it doesn't jolt you from your flow too harshly. You might also set a timer for short breaks, ensuring you don't burn out by working straight through your flexible time.

Accountable in a Flexible World

Self-Monitoring

A flexible schedule doesn't mean zero accountability. At the end of each day, do a quick review. Did you meet the day's important goals? If not, was it because your schedule was too loose, or did you genuinely have unexpected obstacles? Learning from these reflections can help you fine-tune the balance between structure and freedom.

Buddy Check-Ins

Sometimes it helps to have a friend or colleague who also embraces flexible scheduling. You might share your daily anchor points in the morning. By evening, you check in to see if you both stayed on track. This light form of accountability can keep you from drifting too far from your priorities.

Gentle Progress Markers

Even if your schedule flows, you can still mark milestones. For instance, note that you want to see a certain amount of progress in a project by Thursday. As your flexible blocks shift around each day, you'll keep that milestone in mind. If Thursday comes and you haven't hit your target, you might tighten your approach until you catch up.

Knowing When to Get More Rigid

There's a time and place for strict scheduling—like major events or critical deadlines. If your flexible approach isn't cutting it for a particular project, it's okay to switch gears. You might momentarily adopt a stricter routine, scheduling tasks at exact times until the crisis is over. Then you can revert to your easier flow.

The Eternal Battle

Sometimes, life's unpredictability is comedic. You planned a quiet afternoon to catch up on reading, but your neighbor starts power-washing their driveway, or your dog decides this is the moment to practice interpretive dance around your living room. The beauty of a flexible schedule? You can laugh (or groan) and pivot—maybe read in another room, or join your dog's dance routine for a mini-break if you're up for it. The day might not go exactly as intended, but at least you aren't bound by an unyielding timetable.

Making Flexibility a Habit

Small Steps First

If the idea of fewer rules makes you uneasy, start by making just one part of your day flexible. For example, keep your morning routine strict if that helps you feel anchored, but allow your afternoon to be more open-ended. Over time, you might expand that approach to more parts of your schedule.

Reward Yourself for Adjustments

When you successfully adapt to a sudden change without losing your cool— give yourself a quick nod of recognition. That might be as small as a mental "nice job" or as tangible as a short break with a favorite snack. Positive reinforcement helps cement the idea that flexibility can be beneficial, not chaotic.

Communicate Boundaries to Others

If you live or work with people who also rely on your schedule, let them know you're experimenting with a more fluid approach. They might worry you'll become impossible to pin down. Reassure them you still have anchors (like meetings or set times you're available) but that you're leaving wiggle room between tasks. This openness can prevent confusion or frustration if they're used to you running on a tight clock.

Track the Benefits

Every so often, note down specific moments when flexibility saved the day. Maybe you avoided a meltdown by shifting your grocery run to a later slot, or you found an unexpected time to chat with a friend who was in need. These success stories can remind you why flexible scheduling was worth trying in the first place.

Bringing It All Together

A flexible schedule is like a sturdy boat with a little extra slack in the sails, letting you maneuver when the wind changes. You keep a handful of solid anchors—those must-do appointments, family obligations, or personal rituals—but around them, you allow your day to flow. Whether it's buffer blocks, soft deadlines, or overlapping windows, you have options on how and when to get things done.

This approach can be particularly liberating if you have a mind that loves spontaneity or dreads rigid confines. It also acknowledges a universal truth: life rarely cooperates with a minute-by-minute script. Instead, a flexible schedule helps you handle the unexpected gracefully, preserving your sanity and sense of accomplishment.

Sure, it might feel strange at first if you're used to color-coded calendars with every second spoken for. But as you see how easily you can adapt to the day's twists and turns, you'll likely find that your stress levels drop and your productivity doesn't suffer and might even improve.

The ultimate goal is to stay productive and meet your responsibilities without feeling boxed in by a plan that can't bend. Once you experience the freedom of purposeful flexibility, you might wonder how you ever lived without those built-in cushions of space and time.

14

Body Doubling

Ever noticed how, when you do chores or study in the presence of someone else—even if they're not helping—you tend to stay on task longer? This phenomenon, often called "body doubling," taps into our natural drive to mirror or keep pace with the people around us.

Like two friends at a coffee shop, each working on their laptops in silence. They're not necessarily collaborating, but the quiet presence of another person can nudge each one to keep typing, stay focused, and make steady progress. In this chapter, we'll explore why body doubling works, how to make the most of it, and how you can embrace both in-person and virtual options to stay motivated.

Why Body Doubling Works

There's a long-standing notion in psychology called "social facilitation," which says we perform certain tasks better when we sense we're being observed. It's not about pressure or fear—it's more like a mild boost in alertness. If you're alone in a room, it's easy to slip into a daydream or scroll through your phone. But if someone else is nearby—doing their own thing yet also aware of you—you become more aware of yourself. That slight awareness can spark extra determination: "Okay, let me finish this spreadsheet before I check social media."

Mutual Accountability

Body doubling also taps into accountability. Even though the other person might not say a word about your task, you feel a low-key responsibility to keep working. It's like an unspoken agreement: "We're both here to get stuff done, so let's make it happen." For neurodivergent individuals—particularly those with attention challenges—this external anchor helps steady the mind. You're less likely to drift off on a tangent because another set of eyes (or just another presence) anchors you to the task at hand.

Normalizing Work Rhythms

Everyone has a natural work-rest cycle. Some people concentrate in short bursts; others grind away for a solid hour before pausing. Body doubling doesn't force you to match someone else's pace, but it can help you find a comfortable rhythm. If your partner is typing away steadily, you might find yourself matching that energy. Or if they're taking a minute break, it reminds you to do the same. Instead of feeling guilty about breaks, you realize it's part of the process—just done in parallel with someone else.

Connection Minus Pressure

Unlike group projects or collaborations where tasks intertwine, body doubling is typically about parallel work. You each have your to-do list, but you share the same physical or virtual space. There's no competition, no boss-employee dynamic—just a shared understanding that you're both focusing on something. This can relieve the isolation some of us feel when working solo, yet it doesn't trap you in a lengthy team discussion or endless Slack threads. It's the sweet spot between solitude and collaboration.

In-Person Body Doubling

Sitting side by side at a coffee shop with a friend (or a friendly acquaintance) is a classic example of body doubling. You sip your drink, they sip theirs, and each of you tackles your separate tasks. The gentle background noise, occasional eye contact, and presence of another human being can coax you into "work mode." Even if you're not talking, just having another person there can keep you from drifting into a social media vortex. Plus, the mild hum of a public space might give that extra nudge of stimulation some neurodivergent minds crave.

- **Pros:** Easy to arrange, lively atmosphere, minimal planning.
- **Cons:** Can be noisy or crowded, might lead to chatting more than working.

Library Study Buddies

For a quieter setting, libraries are a haven. If you find coffee shops too busy, invite someone to meet at a local library table. You each set up your laptops or books, give a quick nod, and dive into your tasks. The hush of a library can be grounding, and the presence of others who are also studying or reading can reinforce the focus vibe. Even if your buddy takes a break, you remain in an environment that encourages quiet productivity.

- **Pros:** Distraction-free, calm environment, often free WIFI.
- **Cons:** More rules about noise levels, might have limited seating or hours.

Co-Working Spaces

If you're willing to spend a bit (or you work for a company that covers it), co-working spaces offer in-person body doubling on steroids. These spaces are designed for people who want to work around others without necessarily collaborating. You rent a desk, grab a coffee in a shared kitchen, and feed off the collective energy of professionals. If you bring a friend, you've got a built-in accountability partner, but you can also meet new folks aiming to do the same thing.

- **Pros:** Professional ambiance, networking opportunities, stable WIFI.
- **Cons:** Monthly fees, potential for some distracting chatter.

Shared "Chore Sessions" at Home

Sometimes body doubling is about tackling household tasks—folding laundry, cooking, or tidying up. If you have a roommate, partner, or family member, you can plan a shared chore session. You both pick a spot in the house—one person might vacuum while the other organizes shelves—and you keep each other company. The presence of someone else doing chores makes the job less dreary, and it's harder to abandon your tasks for TV if someone else is still working.

- **Pros:** Free, comfortable setting, helps maintain a clean home.
- **Cons:** The potential to chat too much, might lead to distractions like playing with pets or checking the fridge for snacks.

Virtual Body Doubling

Even before global shifts to remote work, some folks discovered that hopping on a video call with a friend or coworker—even if they're muted—can replicate the body-doubling effect. You see each other on screen, maybe give a quick wave, then dive into your tasks. It's surprisingly motivating to glance at the screen and see your friend typing away or reading. You might schedule short check-ins, like "We'll work for 45 minutes, then talk for 5." This method can keep isolation at bay without forcing constant conversation.

- **Pros:** Doesn't require leaving your home, easy to fit into any schedule, works with distant friends.

- **Cons:** Relies on stable internet, can be awkward if there's a big time zone difference, and might tempt you to open more browser tabs.

Online Work Sessions with Strangers

Some online platforms cater to the idea of body doubling with strangers. Think virtual "study rooms" or "focus rooms," where you log in and see video squares of people also aiming to get things done. You might not even learn their names, but you each declare your goal for the session and then work quietly while the camera stays on. It can feel odd at first, but the sense of "We're all in this together" is surprisingly powerful.

- **Pros:** Flexible—join whenever, no prior relationship needed, anonymity can reduce social pressure.
- **Cons:** Comfort level with strangers seeing you, possible varied productivity styles, might feel impersonal.

Team Productivity Tools

Some remote work teams schedule "focus hours" or "group sprints" via Zoom or Slack, where everyone logs on, states their goal, mutes, and checks back in after a set time. This arrangement merges body doubling with accountability, and it works well for short bursts. If you're prone to procrastinating on tedious tasks, a virtual sprint can provide the structure you need: "We'll all do 25 minutes of uninterrupted work, then reconvene to share updates."

- **Pros:** Great for remote teams, fosters camaraderie, easy to implement with existing tools.
- **Cons:** Not as casual as a friend hangout, might feel pressured by the work setting.

Low-Tech Solutions

If the live video feels too intense, you can do a text-based version of body doubling. For instance, you and a buddy might message each other at the start—"I'm working on my resume for the next 30 minutes"—and then check in at the end—"Resume updates done! How about you?" The real-time conversation might be minimal, but knowing you'll update someone can keep you from wandering off to scroll aimlessly. Some folks even do voice-only calls, leaving the line open so they hear the gentle hum of another person breathing or typing.

Making Body Doubling More Effective

Before you start, clarify your goals. Maybe you want to finish reading a chapter, draft a proposal, or tackle the laundry pile. By naming your task—aloud to your partner or typing in a group chat—you set a mini-commitment. This cuts down on aimless drifting because you've told someone what you intend to do.

Time Blocks and Breaks

Body doubling sessions often run best in focused blocks. That could look like the "Pomodoro" approach we discussed in the previous chapters. The break is a chance to chat briefly about progress or vent about a stubborn detail. Then you dive back in. This cyclical pattern can keep you from burning out or drifting off into random YouTube rabbit holes.

Manage Distractions

If you're body doubling in person, agree on ground rules—like minimal social media checks or limiting non-work chat to designated breaks. Virtually, you might keep your microphone muted to avoid picking up background noise or your random commentary. If you must attend to a child, pet, or phone call, let the other person know you'll be back shortly. When you return, reaffirm your task.

Reward Each Other

Sometimes a small pat on the back can go a long way. If you're working with a friend, you might send a quick thumbs-up or "Nicely done!" text when they mention completing a chunk of work. Positive reinforcement can feel great, especially for those who struggle with self-motivation. That said, keep it light—no need to throw a party every time someone sends an email. Balance the encouragement with staying on task.

Set Boundaries

Body doubling isn't a social hour. If you realize you're chatting more than working, it might be time to set a limit. For example: "Let's catch up for 10 minutes, then go quiet for 30." Maintaining that balance ensures you don't drift into an unproductive hangout session. Similarly, if your partner is done early, or if you need extra time, be clear about your decision to continue working or wrap up.

Don't Get Distracted

- **Over-Socializing:** It's tempting to chat away, especially if you get along well. Set an intention: work focus first, small breaks, or a quick wrap-up chat after. If the conversation drags on, gently remind each other why you started.
- **Mismatched Goals:** If you're in a high-energy task but your partner is in a relaxed mood, it can be distracting. Communication helps. Briefly discuss what each of you needs—"I'm doing intense coding, so I'll need quiet." or "I'm just organizing receipts, so I can afford to chat more." Adjust if it's not working.
- **Technology Hiccups:** In virtual sessions, tech can fail—WIFI lags and

software crashes. Have a backup plan. Maybe switch to an audio-only call or reschedule if your internet is having a meltdown. Don't let minor tech troubles become a reason to skip the session altogether.
- **Dependence on the Partner:** Body doubling should boost your productivity, but be cautious about becoming unable to work without it. If you feel stuck whenever your partner is unavailable, gradually try solo sessions. The idea is to build good habits, not rely completely on someone else's presence forever.
- **Unequal Commitment:** Sometimes one person is all-in, while the other is less consistent. That can lead to frustration if you're always showing up on time while your buddy is late. If it becomes a pattern, discuss it. Maybe set a stricter start time or find a new partner if schedules never align.

Making Body Doubling a Habit

If you've never tried body doubling, begin with a short session—maybe 30 minutes. See how it feels. If it's helpful, extend it to an hour or two. You can do it once or twice a week initially. There's no need to jump into daily sessions right away.

Keep a Log or Journal

Note how productive you were during body doubling compared to solo work. Did you accomplish more tasks or feel less stressed? Tracking the difference can motivate you to keep at it and refine your approach.

Combine with Other Tools

You can pair body doubling with other strategies—like color-coded task lists or micro-tasking. For instance, you might break your project into tiny steps (from an earlier chapter's approach), and then tackle them one by one while on a video call. Or if you have a flexible schedule (from another chapter), you can carve out a buffer block specifically for body doubling.

Variety Is Okay

Feel free to switch up your body-doubling partner or environment. Sometimes a single coworker or friend is perfect; other times, it's refreshing to join a virtual room full of strangers focusing on different projects. The novelty can keep things interesting and prevent stagnation.

A Quiet Companion

Body doubling is one of those productivity hacks that seems almost too simple: just have another person around, and magically your focus improves. But behind that simplicity lies a wealth of psychological benefits—accountability, social facilitation, shared energy, and a softer sense of mutual encouragement.

Whether you opt for an in-person setup at the local café, a library table, or a co-working space, or go virtual with video calls and digital co-working rooms, you're tapping into a very human craving for togetherness.

Even though you're not actively collaborating on the same task, you're companionably side by side (physically or virtually), each making progress in your corner of the world. No constant back-and-forth is necessary. Just the knowledge that someone else is working, too. It can help keep distractions at bay, turn a daunting chore into a shared activity, and create a sense of camaraderie even across miles.

Give body doubling a try if you ever feel stuck, isolated, or prone to drifting off mid-task. It's cost-effective (often free), widely accessible (in person or online), and can blend seamlessly with other productivity methods you already use. You might discover that having a quiet companion is exactly what you need to keep your mind from wandering and your motivation from dipping.

And the best part? There's no big meeting or group project required—just you, your work, and one other person, each forging ahead on your separate goals in a shared, supportive space.

15

Timed Transitions

Time can feel slippery—one minute you're replying to an email, and the next thing you know, 45 minutes are gone, lost in a chain of messages, random links, and half-remembered tasks. For many people, especially those with neurodivergent minds, the act of switching from one task to another can cause problems.

You want to move on, but it's easy to get stuck if no clear break or boundary is telling you it's time to stop. That's where timed transitions come in: short countdowns or gentle alerts that signal, "Hey, it's time to shift gears." These countdowns help you avoid "task inertia," the tendency to stay locked on one activity until something (or someone) gives you a push. In this chapter, we'll explore why timed transitions work, how to set them up, and how to ensure they don't accidentally become distractions themselves.

Why Timed Transitions Matter

The Paradox of Staying Too Long

Have you ever watched a short YouTube clip only to discover, an hour later, you've gone down a rabbit hole of recommended videos? That's task inertia at work. You intended to spend 5 minutes, but there was no prompt to pull you away when those 5 minutes expired. Timed transitions act like a visible or audible marker that says, "Time's up for this activity. Now let's shift." Without that nudge, it's too easy to keep scrolling or keep plugging away on the same project, even if it's no longer your top priority.

A Gentle Nudge for Cognitive Shifts

Switching tasks involves changing your mental context—closing files, opening new ones, rewriting mental checklists. If you jump from writing a report to making dinner, that's a lot for your brain to handle in a split second. A short countdown or alert can make this transition smoother. By giving yourself, say, a 2-minute warning, you create a buffer for your brain to wind down from the old task and prepare for the new one. This reduces the friction that often arises when you abruptly end one activity and rush into the next.

Beating Over-Focus and Procrastination

Many neurodivergent individuals have the gift (and curse) of hyper-focus: when they lock onto a task, hours can vanish. Hyper-focus can be amazing for productivity—until it's time to move on but you can't pry yourself away. Conversely, some folks are prone to procrastination: they're so anxious about starting the next item on their list that they linger on the old one (or do something else entirely) to avoid it. Timed transitions offer a middle ground: "I'll give myself until this timer ends, then I have to shift—no second-guessing."

Preserving Energy

Switching tasks repeatedly without a transition strategy can be mentally exhausting, akin to taking off and landing an airplane every few minutes. Each shift demands mental energy to gather new tools or references, recall the next set of requirements, and find your footing. Timed transitions help conserve your limited "switching energy" by providing a predictable, manageable process for letting go of one task and starting another.

The Science of Short Countdowns

Anchoring Attention

When you see or hear a short countdown—like "3, 2, 1, break!"—your attention zeroes in on that marker. This anchors your focus in the present moment, reminding you there's a specific point when you have to stop and switch. If you just rely on your internal sense of time, it's easy to let 3 minutes bleed into 10 or to forget you meant to switch tasks soon. An external anchor (like a timer on your phone, a watch alarm, or a gentle beep from your computer) keeps you accountable.

Triggering Dopamine

Believe it or not, short countdowns can trigger small bursts of dopamine—your brain's "reward" chemical—when the countdown hits zero. Our brains often see countdowns as mini goals, and completing a goal, even a tiny one like "work for 10 more minutes," can give a slight chemical reward. This can provide a sense of closure on the old task, making it psychologically easier to transition.

A Race Against Yourself

Some people find that timed transitions turn routine tasks into quick challenges. If you have 5 minutes left before the alert sounds, you might rush to finish that last paragraph or fold the final bits of laundry, turning the countdown into a mini-race. That added sense of urgency can give you a motivation boost. It also reduces the chance of drifting into "I'll do it later" thinking because you have a ticking prompt nudging you to wrap up now.

Setting Up Timed Transitions

Length of Countdown

A timed transition can be as short as a 1-minute alert or as long as a 15-minute heads-up. The ideal duration depends on how much mental wind-down you need. If you're deep in a complex project, you might like a 5-minute countdown so you can jot down final notes on what you'll do next time. For simpler tasks—like ending a phone call or finishing a light chore—a 1-minute or 30-second alert might suffice. Experiment to see what feels right without intruding on your flow.

Tools and Devices

- **Phone Alarms:** Most smartphones let you set multiple alarms or timers with various sounds. You could label them, too, like "Time to switch from coding to lunch prep."
- **Computer Notifications:** If you're mostly working on a computer, consider browser extensions or productivity apps that can sound alerts or pop-up messages.
- **Wearable Tech:** Smartwatches or fitness trackers often have gentle vibrations for timers, which can be less jarring than a loud beep.
- **Physical Timers:** An old-school kitchen timer or a small digital countdown clock on your desk can do the trick if you prefer a tangible gadget.

Placement and Visibility

Where you place or how you set up your timed transition matters. If it's a phone alarm, is your phone within arm's reach, or is it across the room? If you rely on a software alert, is it easily noticeable or buried behind a dozen browser tabs? Ideally, you want a gentle but clear notification. A subtle approach might be best if you dislike jarring noises—a soft chime, a short vibrate, or a small on-screen pop-up that doesn't block your entire screen.

Tying to Task Completion

One approach is to pair the countdown with the task's scope. For example, "I'll give myself 20 minutes to answer emails, then I'll switch to the next item when the alarm goes off." This method ensures you don't get lost in your inbox for an hour. Another approach is to give a longer block for deep work—maybe 45 minutes—followed by a short 5-minute transition. When that transition alert sounds, you know it's time to stand up, stretch, or quickly jot down what's left to do before changing tasks.

Avoiding Task Inertia

The "One More Thing" Trap

Task inertia sometimes masquerades as "I just need to do one more quick check." That quick check then balloons into 30 minutes. A timed transition helps by setting a firm stop point. You can say, "When the timer dings, I stop—no more last-minute add-ons." If you genuinely need more time, you can manually reset the timer, but at least you're making a conscious choice instead of sliding passively into a longer session.

Mini Previews of the Next Task

If you're reluctant to leave your current task, it might help to mentally preview the next one. When the countdown reaches 2 minutes, think: "Okay, next I'll open that spreadsheet and see if there are any urgent rows." By visualizing what you'll do next, you weaken the inertia chain that holds you to the current task. It's like stepping onto a mental bridge before you fully leave the old task behind.

Using a "Landing Pad"

Some people keep a sticky note or a small text file open as a "landing pad" for undone thoughts. When the timer warns you to wrap up, you quickly jot down any unfinished points so you can pick them up later. This technique reduces anxiety about leaving a task mid-flow. Once you unload your thoughts, you're free to switch without worrying you'll forget something crucial.

In-Person/Virtual Timed Transitions

Working Solo

When you're alone, it's all on you to set up those alerts. The advantage is you have total control—choose the sounds, the intervals, everything. The downside is if you ignore it, there's no one else to nudge you. If you find yourself repeatedly dismissing your timers, you might pair the approach with a friend's check-in or a mild form of accountability, like letting someone know your schedule for the day.

In-Person Teams

If you're collaborating with colleagues or family, you can do a group-timed transition. Maybe everyone agrees to "work heads-down for 25 minutes, then get a 5-minute alert to switch tasks." This fosters a synchronized rhythm. However, you might clash if some folks need more (or less) time. Communicate upfront about how flexible or strict the transition should be.

Remote or Hybrid Work

For distributed teams, you might adopt timed transitions in a virtual co-working session. For instance, you hop on a video call and set a shared timer. Once it rings, everyone quickly updates each other and shifts to a new focus. If you're prone to Zoom fatigue, keep the calls short or use a text-based countdown in a group chat. That way, the entire team sees "5 minutes left" or "Time to switch," but you're not forced to stay on camera.

Using Humor to Ease the Shift

Sometimes task switching can feel abrupt or even comical—like telling a toddler playtime is over. If you add a dash of humor to your timed transition, it can reduce the tension. Maybe your phone alarm is a snippet of a silly tune or the pop-up message says something cheeky like, "Time's up, champion! Go crush the next task!" A small chuckle can make the pivot less jarring, especially if you've been deeply immersed in something serious.

The Sandman's Victims

- **Ignoring or Snoozing Alerts:** It's easy to hit "dismiss." If this becomes a habit, try changing alert sounds or picking a more insistent alarm that makes ignoring it more difficult. Or have a friend or colleague message you if they see you're still on the same task after the timer.
- **Setting Unrealistic Durations:** If you give yourself 10 minutes for a task that needs 30, you'll build frustration. Be realistic in your timing. It's okay to realize mid-way that you need more time—just do so consciously, resetting the timer and acknowledging the extension.
- **Over-Scheduling Transitions:** Too many transitions can break your flow. If your timer goes off every 10 minutes but you're in a deep creative zone, you'll get annoyed. Find a balance. Maybe schedule fewer, longer sessions for tasks that demand immersion and short bursts for repetitive chores.
- **Becoming Timer-Obsessed:** There's a fine line between helpful alerts and feeling like you live by the clock. If you find the constant ticking stressful, scale back. Some tasks might not need a precise countdown; a simpler "around 3 p.m." mental note could suffice.
- **Not Leaving Buffer for Transitions:** If you plan tasks back-to-back with no small gap, even the best countdown won't help. You'll end up behind

schedule if each task takes slightly longer or if you need a real mental shift. Build in small buffers—5 to 10 minutes between blocks—to handle the post-task wrap-up.

Pairing with Other Methods

Body Doubling or Virtual Co-working

We recently explored body doubling: working alongside someone else (in-person or virtually). You can combine that with timed transitions. If you're on a video call, set a shared timer for the session. When it hits zero, everyone transitions together, preventing any one person from pulling the group into extended tangents.

Micro-Tasking

If your tasks are broken into tiny chunks (micro-tasking), timed transitions become even simpler. You assign each micro-task a short block, and when the timer rings, you're done with that chunk—no regrets. This method can be especially useful for tackling big projects in bite-size increments.

Flexible Scheduling

In a flexible schedule, you leave open windows for tasks. Timed transitions can help you pivot within those windows. For example, if you have a 2-hour flex block for errands and writing, you can spend the first 45 minutes on errands, set a 5-minute countdown to switch, and then do 45 minutes of writing. The countdown ensures you don't overdo one part and neglect the other.

Celebrating Progress

Mini-Wins

Every time you successfully follow a timed transition, you're reinforcing a good habit. Acknowledge it. That might be as simple as a mental "Yes, I switched on schedule!" or a quick note in a habit tracker. The more you notice these small wins, the more your brain will seek to repeat them.

End-of-Day Reflection

Take a moment each evening to see how often you stuck to your countdowns. Did you ignore them after lunch? Did you reset one because you needed more time? Observing these patterns helps you refine the process. Maybe you'll realize you need a shorter or longer countdown, or perhaps a gentler or more assertive alert sound.

Sharing Victories

If you have friends or coworkers who also struggle with task transitions, invite them to try this method. You can swap stories about the comedic moments—like "I was in the middle of an online article, the timer beeped, and I closed the tab!" Celebrating these small moments fosters community and encouragement.

Maintaining Momentum Over Time

Revisit Your Timers

As you grow accustomed to timed transitions, you might need to adjust durations. A 20-minute block might have been enough at first, but now you need 30 or even 40. That's fine. The goal is to stay flexible. Adapt the system to your evolving needs rather than forcing yourself to fit an old mold.

Backup Plans

Occasionally, you'll want to intentionally ignore a timer if you're on a roll—maybe you're in the zone writing a paper or finalizing a report. But do so mindfully. Perhaps set a second timer for an extra 10 minutes, telling yourself, "I'll do one final sprint, then definitely switch." This prevents indefinite overrides.

Seasonal or Life Changes

Your day might look different in the summer vs. the winter, or before vs. after a big life event. Don't be afraid to revamp your entire approach for a season. The beauty of timed transitions is that they're easy to shift: new durations, fresh alarm sounds, or different intervals can all keep your workflow feeling fresh and relevant.

Changing Gears Smoothly and Swiftly

Timed transitions act like traffic lights in the day-to-day journey of your tasks. Instead of zooming through intersections (or staying stuck on one road), you get clear signals to slow down, switch lanes, and move on. For many, especially those prone to deep focus or easy distraction, these small countdowns make a huge difference in avoiding inertia.

By using short alerts, you give yourself a gentle heads-up that in 2 minutes, or 5, or 10, it's time to wrap up. This simple practice eases the mental load of switching from one context to another—closing an email thread, saving your current progress, and mentally prepping for the next challenge.

Over time, these transitions become a familiar rhythm, and you'll find you're less likely to resent having to shift gears. You might even start to enjoy the break in pace. Yes, occasional misfires happen—timers can be ignored, software can glitch, or real-life chaos can override your best intentions.

But on the whole, timed transitions act as a helpful guardrail, preventing you from drifting too far off the highway of your daily plan. Pair them with humor, some self-compassion, and a willingness to tweak the process as you go, and you'll likely see improved focus, reduced stress, and greater satisfaction in knowing you can switch tasks smoothly whenever you need.

16

Scheduled Check-Ins

The salty spray stung the captain's face as he gripped the helm, eyes fixed on the horizon. Hours passed, the sun arcing across the sky. But without a compass to read, the ship drifted far from its intended course. Turning back now? A monumental task.

We often navigate our own lives with a similar lack of direction. We set goals, we make plans, but how often do we check if we're still on track? This is where scheduled check-ins come in. Think of them as your personal compass, guiding you toward your true north. They're those essential pauses that allow you to assess your progress and make course corrections before you've veered too far off course.

In this chapter, we'll discover how these check-ins can be your secret weapon for staying focused and achieving your goals, especially for those of us whose minds tend to wander or get captivated by shiny new distractions.

Why Scheduled Check-Ins Matter

Catching Drift Early

It's normal for real-life tasks to take a left turn. Maybe you planned to write a blog post by Friday, but a family event, sudden work demands, or a random burst of Netflix bingeing got in the way. If you never pause to evaluate, you might only discover you're way off track when the deadline hits. A check-in session—whether daily or weekly—lets you spot these derailments early. You can then adjust your timeline or reassign tasks without that last-second panic.

Building Momentum Through Small Steps

Many people, especially those with ADHD or other neurodivergent traits, thrive on consistent feedback. Seeing you've completed even a slice of the job can ignite motivation. Scheduled check-ins provide exactly that feedback loop: each time you pause to measure progress, you confirm what's done and what still needs attention. It's like giving yourself a pat on the back regularly, rather than waiting until the end. Over time, these mini-celebrations can sustain your drive and keep you from burning out.

Reducing Overwhelm

Without periodic check-ins, you might let tasks pile up until they resemble a looming mountain. By the time you see the mountain, it feels too big to tackle. Routine assessments keep things bite-sized: each session, you note what's pending and chip away at it. This steady flow averts the "everything is collapsing" moment. Also, if you notice you're consistently behind schedule, you can lighten your load before it becomes crushing.

Real-Time Adaptation

Life rarely follows the neat path we imagine. New tasks pop up, old tasks become less urgent, or your energy levels shift. Check-ins let you adapt on the fly. Maybe you realize the marketing report you planned is no longer needed, or a sudden personal matter demands more time. Instead of clinging to a rigid plan, you can shuffle priorities and tasks to match current conditions. This adaptability is crucial for staying sane and productive, particularly in a constantly changing environment.

The Anatomy of a Check-In

Frequency and Duration

How often should you stop and assess? There's no one-size-fits-all. Some prefer daily check-ins, others weekly, and still others do both: brief daily reviews plus a more in-depth weekly session. If your tasks are fast-paced or prone to frequent shifts, a short daily check might be essential.

If you're working on long-term projects, a weekly or biweekly deep dive might suffice. Choose a frequency that feels supportive, not nagging. As for duration, these sessions don't have to be long. A quick 5–10 minutes might do wonders for a daily check, while a weekly review might last 30 minutes or more.

Questions to Ask

A good check-in often revolves around simple, direct questions:

- What have I accomplished since the last check-in?
- What obstacles or surprises arose?
- What do I need to prioritize next?
- Is there anything I should remove from my list or delegate?

These prompts shine a light on both achievements and bottlenecks, giving you a clear sense of where you stand. If you find these questions too broad, try sub-questions like "Which tasks are behind schedule?" or "Did I enjoy doing the tasks on my list, or do they drain me?"

Tools and Formats

- **Pen and Paper:** Jotting quick bullet points in a journal or planner. Low-tech but effective for visual people who enjoy crossing things off a page.
- **Digital Task Managers:** If you already track tasks in Trello, Asana, or

another tool, you can do your check-in there. Many apps let you see what's completed and what's overdue, streamlining the process.
- **Audio or Video Notes:** Some find it easier to talk than to write. A voice memo or short video to yourself can capture the essence of your progress without a formal structure.
- **Shared Check-Ins:** If you're part of a team or have an accountability partner, you might hop on a quick call or chat thread to discuss each other's progress.

Setting the Right Tone

A check-in shouldn't feel like a scolding session. Keep it encouraging and solution-oriented. Even if you discover you're behind, focus on how to adapt rather than beating yourself up. The idea is to realign with your goals, not to punish yourself for veering off. **Acknowledge your progress.**

How Check-Ins Help ND Minds

Consistent External Feedback

Many people with neurodivergent minds do better having external prompts and feedback loops—something outside their head that says, "Hey, here's how you're doing." A scheduled check-in can act like a mini anchor in the chaos. By reviewing tasks at set intervals, you get a fresh lens on your progress instead of relying solely on an internal sense of time, which can be skewed by focus or impulsiveness.

Structured Yet Flexible

Rigid systems can feel suffocating, while no system at all might lead to scattered pursuits. Check-ins offer a sweet middle ground. You decide how structured they are: some people like a consistent template of questions, while others prefer a casual conversation with themselves (or a partner).

This structure, combined with the freedom to pivot, resonates well with neurodivergent brains that need both predictability and room to move.

Emotional Regulation

Projects and tasks can stir emotions—anxiety if a deadline is looming, excitement about a new idea, or frustration when stuck. Regular check-ins let you address these emotions before they escalate. For instance, if anxiety about a particular project grows each time you see it on your list, talking it through during your check-in can clarify the real issue and guide you toward the next step or support. It prevents bottled-up stress from exploding at the worst moment.

Preventing Hyper-focus Pitfalls

Hyper-focus can be amazing for deep work, but it can also blind you to other tasks or deadlines. A scheduled check-in is like a built-in alarm that says, "Look up from your work—what else needs attention?" That quick interruption might feel annoying if you're in the zone, but it's a small price to pay to avoid an avalanche of neglected responsibilities later. If you truly need more time in hyper-focus, you can choose to delay or shorten the check-in, but at least you've made an active choice.

Planning Your Check-In Routine

Daily Snapshot

A short daily check-in could happen first thing in the morning or at the end of the workday. In the morning, you might outline what you hope to finish and any looming deadlines. In the evening, you review what happened, celebrate any wins, and note unfinished tasks to carry over. This daily habit is especially helpful if your schedule fluctuates or your energy levels vary.

Weekly Deep Dive

A weekly check-in takes a broader view. You review the major goals or projects, see what was accomplished, and plan the next week's steps. Maybe you track metrics—like how many chapters you wrote, how many tasks you finished, or how many hours you spent on a side hustle. This is also a time to reorder priorities, particularly if something new cropped up midweek or if an older project lost urgency. If you're a fan of color coding or mind mapping, you can incorporate these visuals into your weekly review to see progress at a glance.

Accountability Partner Sessions

If you find it hard to stay disciplined about check-ins alone, consider pairing with a friend, colleague, or coach. You might schedule a quick call every Friday afternoon: each of you lists your top accomplishments, any roadblocks, and next week's targets. This mutual check-in can prevent avoidance—when you know someone's waiting for your update, you're more likely to show up prepared.

Quarterly or Monthly Overviews

Longer intervals, like monthly or quarterly, are for big-picture thinking: Are you heading toward the right goals? Has your vision changed? Should you pivot entirely? These sessions can be more introspective. You might ask, "Is this still what I want to be doing?" or "Have I made measurable strides toward that bigger dream?" Checking in at these wider intervals can keep your daily or weekly tasks aligned with overarching life goals.

Humorous Distractions and How to Handle Them

Check-in sessions can be ironically prone to interruptions. You sit down to review your tasks, and your phone buzzes with a friend's text about last night's TV cliffhanger. Or your dog chooses that moment to bark at a suspicious leaf outside. Or you remember you were supposed to water the plants an hour ago, and you dash off mid-check-in. Embrace the irony. Keep your phone on silent if possible, or adopt a "plant-watering can wait 5 minutes" rule. If your mind wanders mid-check-in, gently steer it back. It's all part of building a habit that your brain recognizes as valuable.

Drift vs. Change

One trick of check-ins is distinguishing between a healthy pivot and aimless drifting. Sometimes you realize a task or project no longer aligns with your bigger goals. Dropping it can be the right call. But sometimes you're just bored or discouraged, and you prematurely abandon ship. A thoughtful check-in process can help differentiate these scenarios. Ask: "Am I switching tasks because it's genuinely outdated or unhelpful, or because I'm impatient or stuck?"

The Pivot Test

During a check-in, if you feel an urge to pivot, consider a quick "pivot test":

- **Revisit the original goal.** Why did you start this project or task?
- **Assess current relevance.** Does that original reason still matter?
- **Evaluate potential gains and losses.** If you pivot, what do you gain (time, energy, new opportunities)? What might you lose (progress, learning, credibility)?
- **Decide with clarity.** If the gains outweigh the losses, pivot with confidence. If not, recommit for another week and reassess later.

Check-Ins With Other Tips

Visual Timers or Alarms

If you're prone to forgetting check-ins, set an alarm on your phone or a visual timer. For daily check-ins, a short beep could remind you each morning or evening. For weekly reviews, you could place a recurring calendar event so you don't accidentally skip it. Even a Post-it note on your laptop—"Review tasks at 4 p.m."—can do the trick.

Micro-Tasks and Check-Ins

If your tasks are already broken down into micro-steps, check-ins can be super easy. You just see which micro-tasks got done. If too many remain undone, you'll know to adjust your approach. By linking micro-tasks to scheduled reviews, you ensure you never let the little steps accumulate into a giant backlog.

Color Coding

Some folks color-code tasks or project statuses (green for on-track, yellow for at-risk, red for overdue). During check-ins, scanning these colors shows you where trouble lurks. You can then focus your pivot on the red or yellow tasks. The simple visual feedback speeds up the decision-making process.

Managing Emotional Responses

Neutral Self-Talk

Check-ins can stir frustration if you see you're behind or didn't accomplish what you planned. Instead of reacting with self-criticism, aim for neutral self-talk: "I'm behind on X. Let's figure out why." The goal is to solve, not to shame. Remember that the act of checking in is a positive step, even if the news isn't great.

Rewarding Small Victories

Spotting even minor progress can lift your mood. If you advance just one step on a project, that's still progress. Progress, not perfection. Acknowledge your progress. Maybe treat yourself to a quick break or a small indulgence: "Hey, I finished drafting the proposal—time for a short walk in the sun." By celebrating incremental wins, you keep your mindset upbeat and engaged.

Asking for Help

Sometimes check-ins reveal persistent roadblocks—like a technical skill gap or a resource you lack. Don't hesitate to seek help, whether from a friend, a mentor, or online forums. The check-in is your signal: "I'm stuck here, so maybe it's time to get input or delegate." Taking that step can turn a frustrating cycle into a breakthrough.

Staying on Track

- **Overthinking the Process:** If you spend more time designing check-in rituals than actually doing them, you've gone too far. Start small and refine as you go.
- **Ignoring Check-In Findings:** It's one thing to note "I'm behind," but if you never shift your schedule or reduce tasks, you'll remain stuck. Each check-in should lead to at least one small tweak or confirmation.
- **Unrealistic Goals:** If every check-in reveals the same story of "didn't get it done," your expectations might be off. Use the check-in to reset goals to a more achievable level.
- **Comparing to Others:** A check-in is about your progress, not your neighbor's. Resist the urge to measure yourself against a friend's to-do list. Everyone's life context is different.
- **Feeling Guilty for Changing Course:** Pivoting or scrapping tasks can be

healthy. Don't let a sense of "I must finish everything I start" trap you in pointless tasks. Check-ins exist to free you from those illusions.

One Check-In at a Time

Scheduled check-ins might sound like a small habit—just a few minutes of review—but they pack a powerful punch. By consistently pausing to see where you stand, you'll catch mistakes or slowdowns sooner, adapt with less stress, and sustain a clearer sense of direction. It's like tapping the brake lightly instead of waiting to slam on it right before a traffic jam.

The key is to keep it simple, consistent, and positive. Whether it's a quick bullet-point list each morning or a weekly deep dive with color-coded tasks, the purpose is the same: reorient yourself, acknowledge what's done, and plot the next step. Especially if you're prone to daydreaming, forgetting deadlines, or chasing new shiny ideas, these regular check-ins function like your friendly co-pilot, reminding you of the route you set.

Over time, you'll find that drifting off course becomes less common. When life's storms come—and they will—your scheduled check-ins act like a rudder, giving you small course corrections so you don't end up far from the destination you intended. And if your destination changes? That's okay, too. By checking in, you'll pivot sooner rather than later, saving time and energy in the long run.

17

Customize Your Routine

Do you ever feel at your best in the morning—typing away, tackling tasks with gusto—only to hit a midday slump that leaves you staring at your screen, wondering where your motivation went? Or maybe you're the opposite, dragging through mornings while your brain lights up at 10 p.m.

Everyone's energy flows in unique patterns, yet we often force ourselves into a single mold prescribed to us: the 9-to-5, one-size-fits-all schedule. That approach can make sense for some, but it can also backfire if it clashes with our natural rhythms. In this chapter, we'll explore how to tune into your personal high and low energy times, then shape a routine that plays to your strengths rather than fights them. Along the way, we'll keep things light and flexible—just like a good schedule should be.

Customizing Your Routine Matters

Our energy isn't static. It ebbs and flows throughout the day in response to biology, sleep patterns, and even sunlight. If you're neurodivergent, these fluctuations might be even more pronounced. Some people experience a big concentration surge in the early morning. Others feel their most alert mid-afternoon, and still others come alive after sunset.

By aligning tasks with these natural peaks and dips, you're not just boosting productivity—you're also reducing mental strain. Imagine trying to push a car uphill versus rolling it along a flat road: one approach is easier.

Battling "One-Size-Fits-All" Schedules

Society often champions the idea of early mornings as the pinnacle of virtue, but that doesn't work for everyone. Some do indeed perform best at dawn; others can't string two words together until they've had lunch. If you fall into the latter category, trying to force an early-bird routine might lead to frustration and guilt.

Instead, customizing your routine means carving out a system that respects your natural inclinations. You trade in the sense of "I must be broken because I can't do mornings" for "I do my best thinking after 3 p.m., so that's when I'll schedule deep work."

Preserving Mental and Emotional Energy

When tasks align with your energy highs, they feel less daunting. Instead of wading through mental fog during your slump, you tackle big projects at times when your brain is ready to fire on all cylinders. This approach can also reduce stress.

If you consistently fight your body's signals—like trying to hold a study session at midnight when you're exhausted—you're more likely to experience burnout. By customizing, you create a routine that's kind to your mind, keeping frustration at bay and freeing up emotional energy for other pursuits.

Room for Life's Chaos

A well-customized routine isn't a rigid timeline. It's more like a map guiding you to do certain tasks when your energy or mood is right. That doesn't mean every day goes perfectly. Surprises happen—your dog might need an emergency vet visit, or a friend might pop by unannounced.

But if you generally aim to fit tasks into windows that match your high or low energy, you'll recover more easily from disruptions. You'll also feel less guilt about moving things around since you know your baseline routine is flexible enough to handle hiccups.

Finding Your Patterns

Start with a basic approach: track how you feel at different times of the day. You can jot notes in a journal or use a phone app that reminds you to label your energy level and mood every couple of hours. After a week, look for patterns—maybe you're consistently a 3/10 right after lunch, or you peak around 9 a.m. with an 8/10 rating. These observations can guide you toward scheduling tasks during your prime hours.

Digital Tools for Rhythm Tracking

If you like data, wearable devices or apps can track your sleep cycles, heart rate, and even mild body movements to estimate when you're most alert. Some productivity apps also log your keyboard or mouse activity to see when you're active.

You don't have to rely exclusively on such data, but it can confirm hunches. If you suspect your best window is mid-morning, the app might show that's when you're doing the most keystrokes.

Trying Time Experiments

Another option is to conduct short experiments: for one week, handle complex tasks in the morning; the next week, try them mid-afternoon. Compare your outcomes. Did you produce better work, finish faster, or feel less exhausted in one time slot over the other? These mini-experiments let you test assumptions about your natural rhythms.

You might discover that you function best for creative thinking around 11 p.m., so that's when you write, and you reserve chores and errands for midday when your focus is mediocre anyway.

Listening to Your Emotions

Energy isn't just physical. Emotional and mental energy matter, too. Some days your mind might buzz with fresh ideas; other days, you wake up feeling heavy. Pay attention to these cues. If your mind is sluggish but your body is restless, maybe that's a sign to do something physical—like chores or errands—instead of intense cognitive tasks. If your heart feels excited and imaginative, that's the perfect moment to brainstorm or tackle a creative project.

Matching Tasks to Energy Levels

Identify which jobs demand maximum focus, creativity, or problem-solving. These belong in your high-energy slots. It might be coding a complex program, writing an essay, or brainstorming a new marketing strategy. During these tasks, avoid distractions and lean into your natural momentum. Think of it as saving your prime time for the stuff that needs it.

Medium-Energy Tasks

Some activities require attention but aren't as mentally taxing—responding to routine emails, reviewing documents, or doing surface-level research. Place these in a time slot when you're moderately alert. You don't need your absolute peak, but you shouldn't be half-asleep either. This approach avoids "wasting" prime mental hours on tasks that don't demand it.

Low-Energy Tasks

When you're in a slump, aim for simpler tasks: data entry, light cleaning, or mindless errands. Don't beat yourself up if you can't do deep work during a dip. Instead, plan for these times. If 2 p.m. is always a lull, schedule some easy filing or a quick walk outside to reset. Even better, you might do something physical if your brain is tired but your body can still move. That way, you're still accomplishing something without forcing mental acrobatics.

Built-In Breaks

Regardless of how well you allocate tasks, energy is finite. Schedule short breaks or switch tasks before you hit a total crash. If you ride the wave of productivity until you're drained, the recovery can be longer. Brief pauses—like a quick stretch, a snack, or a chat with a friend—help maintain momentum. This is especially true if you're neurodivergent and your focus can go from 100 to 0 in a flash. Small, planned pit stops often work better than pushing until you collapse.

Crafting a Personalized Routine

A flexible yet organized routine might include anchors (fixed points in your day) and flex blocks. Anchors could be mealtimes or standing commitments, like a daily team meeting at 10 a.m. Around these anchors, you insert flex blocks that match your energy cycles.

For example, if you're an early riser, you might block 7–9 a.m. for focused work, then plan an easy chore or break around 9–10 a.m. (the anchor meeting). After that, you might have another high-focus period if you're still buzzing, or a lower-energy block if your momentum dips.

Experimenting with Start Times

If your life allows, try shifting your start or end times. Some workplaces offer flexible hours, so you can begin earlier or later. If you're sharper in the afternoon, request a 10 a.m. start. If mornings are your jam, ask for a 7 a.m. start. Even if you're freelancing or working from home, you can experiment by starting your main tasks at different times each day, noticing where you feel best.

Seasonal Adjustments

Your energy might change with the seasons—longer daylight in summer vs. shorter, darker days in winter. Instead of forcing the same routine year-round, adapt. In winter, you might schedule intense tasks at midday when the sun's out (to stave off drowsiness).

In summer, maybe you get up earlier to enjoy cooler morning air or shift tasks to cooler evenings. Recognizing these shifts helps you avoid frustration when your usual schedule stops working around January.

Keeping Life Goals in View

While customizing your routine, ensure it aligns with bigger life goals. If fitness is a priority, maybe you want to schedule a brisk walk or gym session during your mid-afternoon slump to recharge. If family time matters, block out a chunk in the evening to be fully present. A good routine doesn't just revolve around maximizing productivity—it also respects the personal joys, relationships, and well-being you value.

Staying Motivated When Routine Changes

Customizing your routine is an ongoing process, not a one-time fix. Life events, new jobs, changing seasons, or even health issues can shift your energy patterns. Don't view every deviation as a failure.

Embrace the idea that routines evolve. If you discover your newly minted schedule isn't working, tweak it. That's progress, not an error. By now you probably know what I'm going to say. **Acknowledge your progress.**

Celebrate Small Wins

When you manage to do a challenging task at your energy peak and it flows easily, note that success. Maybe you soared through a writing session at 9 a.m. because you finally realized that's your sweet spot. Congratulate yourself—

it's a sign you're aligning tasks with natural rhythms. A quick mental "yes!" or small reward (like a favorite snack) can keep you enthusiastic about refining your routine.

Taking a Lighthearted Attitude

Sometimes people treat scheduling like a serious, no-jokes-allowed affair. But routine-building can be fun, especially if you let yourself laugh at the quirks. Maybe you realize you have a random surge of energy at 11:47 a.m. daily. It's kind of weird, right? Chuckle at it and plan a short "power quarter-hour" for 11:47–12:02. Leaning into these oddities can bring a sense of playfulness and reduce stress.

Checking In Regularly

Routines can drift without you noticing, so do occasional check-ins (like we discussed in the previous chapter). Ask, "Is my schedule still matching my energy? Are mornings still my best focus time?" If not, adjust. This flexibility ensures you don't fall into a rut by keeping the routine fresh and effective.

Practical Tips for Smooth Transitions

Remember those cues from a couple of chapters ago? They work here. When it's time to shift from one energy-based slot to another, maybe you set a gentle alarm on your phone or watch. Or place a sticky note near your workspace saying "Afternoon slump? Do chores or errands now." Some prefer a quick stretch or musical cue—like playing a short, upbeat song to mark the shift from high-focus to low-focus activity.

Building In Ramps

If you're about to tackle a high-focus task but feel a bit scattered, do a short "ramp-up" activity: review your notes, gather necessary materials, or do a quick mental warm-up. Similarly, when winding down a low-energy task before a break, you might do a "ramp-down" by saving your progress, tidying your space, or setting a mini-goal for the next session. These ramps ease you in and out of different energy modes.

Watch Out for Over-stimulation

If you're neurodivergent and easily overstimulated, be mindful of how you schedule tasks around your peaks. For instance, if you're super alert in the afternoon, you might also be more sensitive to noise or visual chaos. If that's the case, try to work in a quieter environment or use headphones. Conversely, if you're prone to feeling sluggish, a bit of background noise or a co-working environment could perk you up.

Avoiding All-Or-Nothing Thinking

Some days, your normal "high-energy" period might feel sluggish because you didn't sleep well or you're stressed. That doesn't mean your entire system is broken. See it as a temporary fluctuation. You could still attempt your important tasks, but give yourself grace. If it's not working, shift your schedule for that day. The routine is a guide, not a chain.

Don't Complicate It

- **Over-complicating the Schedule:** Customizing doesn't mean scheduling every 15-minute block. Keep it broad: identify your high, medium, and low times, then assign tasks accordingly. If you go overboard with color-coded grids, you may spend more time planning than doing.
- **Ignoring Real-World Constraints:** Sometimes you have to show up at 8

a.m. because your boss insists, or you can't run errands in the evening because stores are closed. If external factors limit your ideal routine, focus on adjusting the parts you can control. Maybe the hour before bedtime can still be your creative space.
- **Punishing Yourself for "Off Days":** Everyone experiences days where the usual pattern fails, whether due to poor sleep, illness, or unexpected stress. Don't toss your entire routine if a single day collapses. Instead, see it as an outlier. If it becomes frequent, reevaluate your approach.
- **Comparing to Others:** Your best friend might swear by 5 a.m. workouts, but if that schedule leaves you groggy, why force it? Resist the temptation to mimic someone else's routine just because it works for them. We all have different bodies, minds, and responsibilities.
- **Not Updating as You Grow:** Routines that work when you're a student might fail when you have a 9-to-5 job or a family. Big life changes—new job, moving, health issues—can alter your energy patterns. Check in every few months or after major changes to see if your routine still fits.

Maintaining a Sustainable Rhythm

A customized routine works better when underpinned by good sleep, nutrition, and movement. If you're ignoring self-care, no schedule will magically fix your fatigue. Make sure your plan accounts for rest days, breaks, and meal times. If your energy is consistently low, it might be a sign you need to fine-tune your sleep or talk to a medical professional.

Accountability Partners

It can be helpful to share your routine experiments with a friend or colleague. Maybe you both decide to tackle challenging tasks in the early afternoon, then text each other to confirm you're doing it. Or you commit to a buddy that you won't schedule heavy mental tasks at night if it leads to insomnia. This bit of friendly oversight can keep you honest and help you refine your approach.

Adapt, Don't Abandon

If you find a certain arrangement isn't working, tweak it. Perhaps your high-energy window is shorter than you thought, or your mid-afternoon slump hits sooner. It's not an all-or-nothing deal. You might shift your prime tasks 30 minutes here or there until you pinpoint the sweet spot. Over time, you'll build confidence that you can flex and flow instead of feeling locked into a failing plan.

Celebrate Progress

When you align tasks with your energy, you'll likely see improvements: fewer frustrated hours, less pushing yourself uphill, and more tasks completed with relative ease. Notice these wins. Say to yourself, "My new approach to scheduling creative work after dinner works!" Let that sense of victory fuel further experimentation. We're after progress, not perfection, right? So acknowledge your progress.

Respecting Your Natural Flow

Customizing your routine isn't about chasing a mythical "perfect schedule." It's about understanding your highs and lows and playing to those strengths. By identifying which hours your mind and body feel most capable—and which times are best for lighter tasks or rest—you establish a framework that makes each day less of a struggle and more of a collaboration with your rhythm.

Yes, life will still throw curve-balls. You might have to attend an early meeting despite being a night owl, or you might find yourself wide awake at midnight when you'd planned to sleep. But when your baseline routine respects your nature, these disruptions don't derail you as much. You can adapt quickly, returning to your chosen rhythm once the storm passes.

So permit yourself to break away from the strict 9-to-5 or the default "morning is best" mindset. Track your energy, experiment with time slots, and see what genuinely works. Over the long run, customizing your routine can enrich not just your productivity but your overall well-being.

Instead of constantly fighting yourself, you'll find a smoother path—one that harnesses the ebb and flow of your energy rather than pushing against it.

18

One Priority at a Time

In your mind, place yourself in a busy kitchen during the dinner rush: pots bubbling, pans sizzling, orders called out left and right. Easily getting overwhelmed if you try to stir every pot at once. Yet in our everyday lives—between emails, text messages, social media feeds, and errands—many of us treat each day like that frantic kitchen.

Single-tasking offers a calmer alternative: focusing on one priority at a time, fully immersing yourself in that task before moving on to the next. In this chapter, we'll explore how single-tasking can ramp up the depth and quality of your work, while also preserving your energy. We'll also share strategies for shutting out distractions, so you can concentrate on what truly matters.

Why Single-Tasking Beats Juggling

For years, multitasking was hailed as the path to super-productivity, like having eight arms in that imaginary kitchen. In reality, science says our brains rarely do two things at once. Instead, we switch rapidly between tasks, draining mental energy with each flip.

This constant "task-switching tax" can lead to sloppy errors, repeated steps, or forgetting crucial details. It also leaves us feeling frazzled, like we've run a marathon without ever hitting a stride. By focusing on one priority, you stop paying that tax. You give your mind the room to settle into a task instead of scrambling between competing demands.

A Deeper Level of Engagement

When you concentrate on a single activity, you often enter a "flow" state—an immersive zone where you become so absorbed that time passes almost unnoticed. This state enhances creativity and problem-solving. Think of it like diving deep underwater: you see the details that get lost when you're skimming the surface.

If you've ever noticed how reading a novel in one sitting draws you into the story, or how focusing on a puzzle for an hour leads to sudden insights (even those unrelated to said puzzle), that's single-tasking in action. It lets you savor the nuances and produce higher-quality work.

Never-ending Swirling

Neurodivergent minds, in particular, can feel overwhelmed by the endless swirl of tasks and thoughts. Single-tasking acts as a calm center in the storm. Instead of trying to keep track of every pot on the stove, you settle on one. This can minimize stress because you're not juggling mental to-do lists mid-task. It also prevents the mental clutter that builds when you keep half an eye on your inbox, another on your phone notifications, and a third on the actual task at hand.

Stronger Follow-Through

When you commit to focusing on a single task, you raise the likelihood of finishing it. Many of us start projects with enthusiasm, only to drop them midway when new tasks pop up like bright shiny objects.

By intentionally blocking out distractions and devoting your attention to one thing, you strengthen the "follow-through" muscle. This consistent approach fosters confidence too—each completed item signals, "Yes, I can do this," fueling motivation for the next round.

Shutting Out Distractions

Your phone buzzes: a random group chat meme, a push alert from a shopping app, an email you don't need to read until tomorrow. Each ping can break your concentration for minutes. If you're committed to single-tasking, review your notification settings. Disable or mute anything that isn't crucial.

You can still check social apps later during breaks, but choose the timing yourself instead of reacting to every beep. If silence makes you uneasy, use do-not-disturb modes that still allow calls from specific people or contain emergency alerts.

Set "Do Not Disturb" Blocks

Some phone and computer software allows scheduling do-not-disturb blocks. You can designate, say, 10–11 a.m. as "no notifications," letting you immerse in a project. If you worry about missing something urgent, you can whitelist important contacts like family members or your boss.

This approach ensures you won't hear about a flash sale or a social media mention until after your block ends. It's like closing a door on the digital hallway outside your workspace.

Browser Extensions for Focus

If your main distractions come from the web—like reading news articles or random browsing—try extensions that block or limit certain sites during work sessions. You can set up "focus modes" that only allow essential websites (like references or research portals), while social media or entertainment sites remain off-limits until you manually switch off the block.

It might feel draconian at first, but removing temptation can help you form new habits. Over time, you'll rely less on these tools as your single-tasking mindset strengthens.

De-clutter Your Workspace

Messy desks can mirror messy minds. If you see random mail, half-finished knitting projects, or last week's coffee cups, your eyes might wander from the task at hand. Try to keep your immediate work area minimal—just the tools you need for the current priority.

That might mean storing extra materials in drawers or shelves, away from sight. You don't have to be a neat freak, but a relatively clean surface helps reduce visual distractions.

Manage Noise Levels

Some thrive with background noise (like a coffee shop hum), while others need absolute quiet. Figure out which environment helps you single-task best. Noise-canceling headphones or a white noise machine can be a blessing if you're easily distracted by random sounds.

Conversely, if total silence feels unnerving, you might opt for ambient music or a low-level hum of conversation. The key is to avoid letting a bustling environment constantly steal your attention.

Visual Signals

For those who share space with others—roommates, family, or coworkers—visual signals can help. Maybe you place a colored sign on your desk that says, "Focusing—please let me work." Or you wear noise-canceling headphones as the universal "do-not-disturb" sign. *Unless you're talking about my kids, for some reason they haven't understood the assignment.* This isn't about being rude; it's about safeguarding your single-tasking zone. If someone needs you, they can politely knock or wait until your sign is down.

Protecting Mental Boundaries

Before diving into a single-task session, define exactly what you want to accomplish. "I'll draft two sections of the report" or "I'll fold this load of laundry." Having a specific goal anchors your mind. If your thoughts start drifting to "I should check email," you can remind yourself that you intend to finish the report sections. This mental anchor helps you resist the urge to jump tasks mid-stream.

Use Timed Sessions

Short, intense bursts (like the Pomodoro Technique we've discussed) can be a great fit for single-tasking. You work on one thing for 25 minutes, then take a 5-minute break. The idea is that during those on-periods, you do not waver.

If you recall something else you need to do, jot it down on a notepad and return to your main task. Knowing you'll have a break soon can ease the panic of "I might forget that other thing," because you'll address it in your designated break time.

Let Go of Multitask Guilt

Some of us feel pressured to juggle everything at once, thinking it proves our efficiency. But single-tasking is not laziness; it's a strategic focus. If you catch yourself feeling guilty—like "I should also be vacuuming while on this conference call"—pause and question that assumption.

Doing two half-baked jobs simultaneously is rarely better than doing one thoroughly. Remind yourself that the benefits of single-tasking—less stress, deeper engagement, higher quality—often outweigh the fleeting thrill of "Look, I'm multitasking!"

The Benefits of Single-Tasking

When you give a single task your undivided attention, you notice subtleties you'd otherwise miss. Whether it's writing code, designing a new layout, or solving a tricky homework assignment, your brain gets the chance to dig in without interruption.

This fosters deeper insights because you're not pulling your mental resources away every time a notification dings. Complex problems often require mental "incubation," and single-tasking provides that environment more readily.

Improved Accuracy

Multitasking can lead to small slips—typos in an email, missing detail in a calculation, or forgetting a crucial instruction from a client. By single-tasking, you reduce these slip-ups.

You can proofread thoroughly, double-check data, or confirm steps without the mental residue from a half-dozen other tasks swirling in your head. Over time, building a reputation for quality and accuracy often pays off, whether at school, work, or personal projects.

Enhanced Enjoyment

It's not all about productivity metrics. Single-tasking often makes tasks more enjoyable because you're fully present. Think about reading a good book without glancing at your phone, or cooking a meal while truly savoring the chopping and stirring.

This presence can turn even mundane tasks into mini-meditations. You might find unexpected satisfaction in folding laundry or organizing a closet if you let yourself sink into the flow instead of dividing your attention.

Confidence Boost

Finishing tasks feels great. (Hello, dopamine!) Finishing them well, with full immersion, feels even better. Each time you complete a job to the best of your ability, you reinforce a sense of competence. That confidence can ripple into other areas of your life, from tackling bigger challenges to speaking up in meetings. It's like telling yourself, "I can commit to something and see it through," which beats the chaotic feeling of half-finishing multiple tasks.

Resistance to Single-Tasking

Sometimes, switching tasks feels good. Maybe you've hit a frustrating spot in your current project, and diving into something else is a relief. Recognize that desire for novelty, but see if you can push through it. Often, the best breakthroughs happen after a momentary struggle. If it's truly untenable, set a short break or micro-task to refresh, but commit to returning afterward.

Fear of Missing Out (FOMO)

We worry that if we ignore emails or chats, we'll miss something urgent. In reality, most messages can wait a bit. If your profession demands real-time responses, you could set a compromise: half-hour single-task sessions, then a quick check of your inbox. Over time, you'll likely realize that real emergencies are rare, and the trade-off is worth it: you protect your focus and deliver higher-caliber results.

Anxiety About Large Projects

When faced with a large, intimidating project, single-tasking can feel like you're staring at a mountain with no rope. To handle this, break the mountain into smaller hills (micro-tasks). Devote each single-task session to one micro-step. For example, if you're writing a research paper, one session might be "gather references," and the next might be "draft introduction."

This approach ensures you're not overwhelmed by the entire mountain at once.

Peer or Cultural Pressure

In some workplaces, multitasking is mistakenly seen as a badge of honor. Colleagues might brag about answering emails during meetings or balancing multiple projects at the same hour. Politely hold your ground. If single-tasking improves your output, you have a strong argument for maintaining focus. Communicate that you're not lazy or uncooperative—you're simply applying a proven strategy to do your best work.

Setting Up Single-Tasking Routines

Even if your day is chaotic, aim for a couple of single-task blocks. Maybe it's 30 minutes after breakfast or an hour in the evening. During these blocks, commit fully to one priority. Over time, you can expand if you find it beneficial. The key is consistency—let your mind learn that these blocks are sacred focus time.

Checklists to Channel Focus

When you start a single-task session, have a micro-checklist from Chapter 8: step 1, step 2, step 3. It keeps your mind from wandering—each item acts like a stepping stone. If you're writing a blog post, for example, your list might read "(1) Outline main points, (2) draft introduction, (3) write body paragraphs." If your attention drifts, glance at the list and see which stone you're on.

Prepare to Pause Other Tasks

If you're working in a role that can't fully ignore incoming tasks—like customer support—arrange minimal coverage or away status. Let coworkers know you're focusing for 30 minutes, but they can message you for true emergencies. That way, you're not anxious about ignoring something crucial, yet you're not letting every minor ping shatter your concentration.

Don't Disappear, Though

- **Rigid Single-Tasking:** Sometimes, tasks naturally overlap: cooking dinner while a pot simmers might let you tidy the kitchen. That's okay if it's a logical pairing. Single-tasking shouldn't become so extreme that you ignore practical, minor combos. Just be honest about which combos help rather than hinder.
- **Overly Long Focus Sessions:** If you set a 3-hour block for a single task, you may burn out halfway. Break it up with short stretches or water breaks. Single-tasking doesn't mean chaining yourself to a chair until you collapse.
- **Forgetting External Deadlines:** Focusing on one project is great, but don't neglect a second, urgent project. Balance your schedule so that single-task blocks address all priorities over time, not just the one you prefer.
- **Burnout from Intense Sessions:** High-intensity focus can be mentally draining. If you feel wiped out after a single-task block, integrate some gentler tasks or downtime next. This helps you recharge rather than plow forward in a haze.
- **Ignoring Life Context:** If you have kids or care-giving duties, you can't always single-task at will. Adapt to your life stage. Maybe 20-minute bursts are all you can manage. That's still better than none. Over time, you might find creative solutions, like swapping childcare with a neighbor for an hour, so you get undisturbed time.

Building Depth into Your Daily Life

Single-tasking represents more than a productivity hack; it's a mindset shift. By choosing to focus on one priority at a time, you invite greater depth into everyday experiences. Instead of rushing through tasks, you give each one the attention it deserves. That approach can spill over into hobbies, relationships, and even relaxation. Watching a movie without browsing your phone might make it more fulfilling. Chatting with a friend without checking texts can deepen your bond. Cooking dinner while truly savoring each step—no scrolling through memes—can transform a routine chore into a satisfying ritual.

Keeping Single-Tasking Sustainable

Every few weeks, pause to assess how single-tasking is going. Are you seeing improved concentration and better work quality? Or are you feeling restless? If you're restless, maybe you need shorter focus blocks or more variety in your day. Adjust as needed. The goal isn't to lock yourself into a rigid system but to harness your attention effectively.

Celebrate Completions

When you wrap up a significant task, celebrate briefly. It could be as simple as stepping away from the computer to enjoy a snack. Acknowledging each single-task success reinforces the habit. You'll remember how good it feels to finish something thoroughly rather than scattering your energy in multiple directions.

Laugh Off Slip-Ups

We're human. Sometimes you'll vow to single-task but find yourself opening a new tab or replying to a friend's text mid-task. Don't spiral into self-criticism. Just calmly close the extra tab or put your phone away. Over time, these moments will become rarer, but only if you maintain a kind sense of humor about your mistakes.

Expand at Your Pace

If single-tasking is new, start small—maybe one or two tasks a day. Once you see how much it helps, you can expand. You might eventually shape most of your work or study sessions around it. That said, remain flexible. Certain tasks or times call for a quick scan of multiple threads, especially if your job demands it. The point is to default to single-tasking when possible, not to force it in every scenario.

One Step (or Task) at a Time

Focusing on one priority at a time is like shining a flashlight on a single part of the path, revealing details you'd miss if you scattered your light across multiple directions. It's about resisting the temptation to "do it all" simultaneously, trusting that depth and thoroughness surpass shallow multitasking in the long run. By setting boundaries, creating a welcoming workspace, and committing to a single goal at a time, you allow your brain to work at its best pace.

It's not always easy, especially in a world that glorifies busyness. But the payoff—less stress, better work, and a calmer mind—makes it worth trying. And remember: single-tasking isn't a straitjacket. Life will still toss you curve-balls, and some tasks do overlap naturally.

The heart of the practice is intentional focus so you can see progress, not perfection. Each time you choose one priority and give it your full attention, you reclaim a bit of your mental territory from the chaos, moving closer to a life where quality trumps the frantic pursuit of quantity.

IV

Environment and Stimulus

The previous part gave us the structure to stay on track, but the spaces around us are just as influential in our productivity. Your environment can manage energy, mood, and focus. In this part, we will look at how surroundings can empower, or undermine, your mind. From battling the chaos of clutter to fine-tuning sensory inputs like noise and lighting, these chapters explore how to craft a space that works for you, not against you.

19

Noise-Reduction Aids

It's a Friday and you've had a busy week. You're trying to concentrate in a bustling café because that was the option this afternoon. A barista shouts out latte orders, someone clinks dishes behind the counter, and a group of friends chat animatedly at the next table. For some with cognitive differences, this background buzz might be a pleasant hum. But for others, especially those sensitive to noise, it can feel like a bombardment.

Our world is loud: cars honking, neighbors mowing lawns, coworkers chattering about their weekend. Noise-reduction aids come to the rescue by giving you more control over your soundscape. In this chapter, we'll explore the different tools—from simple foam earplugs to advanced noise-canceling headphones—that can help you reclaim focus and peace.

Why Noise Matters

Noise doesn't just break your focus at the moment—it can linger, rattling around your mind even after the sound stops. Especially for individuals with ADHD or heightened sensory sensitivity, a sudden loud noise (like a dog barking or a car alarm) can jolt you out of whatever you're doing, making it twice as hard to get back. If constant chatter or random clinks plague you, you might never sink into a flow state. Noise-reduction aids serve as a buffer, letting you stay immersed in your task.

Stress and Over-stimulation

Ongoing noise can feel like mental static, causing fatigue or irritability over time. It's often described as too many channels playing in one's head at once. Think of the difference between a calm ocean wave and a raging storm.

A little background noise might be okay—a few waves lapping the shore—but a continuous roar can overload your senses. By cutting down on that auditory chaos, you reduce stress and free up mental bandwidth. This can boost your mood and help you conserve energy for creative or demanding tasks.

Personal Tolerances Vary

One person might thrive with music blaring, while another can't handle even a whisper while reading. In large part, this is about personal thresholds. Some are "under-sensitive" to noise—they don't notice or mind disruptions. Others are "over-sensitive," picking up every little drip of the faucet. Even still, some need the noise to focus.

Understanding where you stand on this scale helps you choose the right strategies. If mild background noise soothes you, you might not want total silence. But if you're the type who hears a pin drop two rooms away, you'll likely need a stronger solution.

The Link to Mental Health

Constant, unwanted noise can fray your nerves, leading to higher anxiety or even heightened anger. Over time, this can affect your mental well-being. Quiet moments let your mind reset. Many find that a calmer soundscape helps them manage mental health concerns by reducing sensory triggers. Adding noise-reduction aids to your routine might be as beneficial as meditation or a good night's sleep in stabilizing your mood.

Figuring Out Your Noise Triggers

Not all sounds bother everyone equally. For some, it's human voices—your coworkers' chatter, a friend's TV in the next room, a neighbor's phone call, the sound of someone chewing. Others might struggle more with mechanical or repetitive noises: humming air conditioners, ticking clocks, or barking dogs.

Track your reactions for a few days. Note when you feel especially irritated or distracted. Is it random car horns? Squeaky chairs? This record helps you pinpoint problem noises so you can address them specifically, rather than blasting all sound out of existence.

Time-of-Day Factors

Sometimes noise triggers are tied to certain times. For instance, traffic might be worst in the morning, or a roommate might watch loud TV after 9 p.m. By noticing these patterns, you can plan your quiet tasks (like reading or focusing on a project) around the quieter hours, or use noise-reduction tools specifically when you know the noise is at its peak. If your neighbor always mows the lawn at 7 a.m. on Saturdays—well, that might be your cue to put in earplugs if you want to sleep in.

Environmental Shifts

Even "safe" environments can surprise you. A typically quiet office might turn chaotic if there's a sudden meeting or if someone brings their toddler to visit. If your local café is calm on weekdays but jam-packed on Fridays, that's worth noting. By staying aware of these fluctuations, you can adjust your schedule or bring along gear (like headphones) to handle unexpected spikes in noise.

Emotional Overlays

Sometimes noise is more irritating when you're already stressed or tired. That faint hum you barely noticed on a good day might drive you up the wall after a rough morning. Recognize that your emotional state can amplify or reduce how noise affects you. This awareness can guide you to be more patient with yourself. If you're in a fragile mood, maybe it's best to avoid a busy location or use stronger noise protection that day.

Noise-Canceling Headphones

Noise-canceling headphones use microphones and clever audio processing to create a counter-sound that neutralizes incoming noise. It's like two waves canceling each other out. They don't always eliminate 100% of the sound, especially higher-pitched or sudden noises, but they significantly cut droning sounds like airplane engines, office air conditioners, or distant traffic. Many models also let you switch between full cancellation and a "transparency" mode, so you can hear if someone talks to you directly.

Picking the Right Pair

You don't have to spend a fortune, although premium brands often offer better cancellation and comfort. Look for headphones that fit well without pinching. Consider battery life if you plan on using them for long stretches. Some have added features like built-in voice assistants or touch controls—nice but not essential if all you need is quiet. If possible, test them in-store or read reviews about how they handle everyday noises, not just airplane travel.

Maintaining Awareness

One caution: wearing noise-canceling headphones can make you oblivious to your surroundings. This can be unsafe in public spaces, especially near roads or while walking. If you need situational awareness, lower the noise-canceling level or use partial noise reduction. Also, if you share a home, it's wise to let people know you can't hear them, so they don't assume you're ignoring them. A polite "I'm wearing headphones—tap my shoulder if you need me" can spare confusion.

Durability and Care

Noise-canceling tech can be fragile—frequent drops or exposure to moisture might degrade performance. Keep them in a protective case when not in use, and clean earcups gently. Over time, you might need to replace ear cushions if they wear out. With good care, they'll last longer and keep providing that sweet hush you crave.

Other Noise-Reducing Options

Sometimes simple foam earplugs do the job. They're cheap, widely available, and easy to carry around. There are also specialized earplugs for musicians or people with noise sensitivity. These filters reduce volume without muffling sound quality too much.

So if you're attending a concert or working in a shared office, these can help lower the decibel level without isolating you completely. For everyday tasks at home—like reading or writing—foam earplugs might be enough if you just need a quiet bubble.

White Noise Machines

A white noise machine (or an app on your phone) generates a consistent sound that masks other noises. Think of it as static, ocean waves, or gentle rainfall. The constant background helps your brain tune out unpredictable sounds like people talking in the hallway.

Some prefer pink or brown noise variants, which have different frequencies and can be more soothing, especially for some in the neurodivergent tribe who find true white noise too harsh. Experiment with various soundscapes—

rainfall, fan sounds, forest ambiance—to see which is least distracting for you.

Sound-Dampening Panels or Curtains

If you have a room where noise seeps in, adding acoustic foam panels on walls or thick curtains can reduce echoes and external noise. You won't magically turn your home office into a recording studio, but it can cut down on reflections and muffle outside sounds.

Heavy rugs on hardwood floors help absorb noise. If you rent, you might not be able to do major soundproofing, but small steps—like a draft stopper under the door or thick tapestries on walls—can make a difference.

Creative DIY Solutions

In a pinch, you can improvise. Stacking pillows or cushions against a shared wall might slightly muffle a chatty neighbor. If you have a noisy appliance, placing a piece of foam or rubber mat underneath could reduce vibration. Even rearranging furniture to block a direct sound path helps a bit. These small tweaks can add up. If you're on a tight budget, get inventive with your environment—sometimes an old blanket behind a door is all you need to tame noise a little.

Matching the Tool to the Noise

A big difference is whether your environment produces steady noise—like traffic hum—or random bursts—like a coworker popping balloons for no reason at all (hey, it happens; can't tell you why, but it does). Noise-canceling headphones or white noise machines excel at handling steady droning.

Sudden sounds are trickier. You might prefer earplugs or a quick gesture to slip on headphones the moment you sense a potential burst. Or you might accept that some sudden noises will penetrate the barrier, but at least you're protected from the general background.

Industrial-Strength Protection

If you work on a construction site or near heavy machinery, consider professional-grade earmuffs designed to meet safety standards. They often look bulky but protect your hearing from dangerously loud decibels. Even outside of formal workplaces, if you're operating loud tools (like leaf blowers or saws) at home, these earmuffs can save you from hearing damage. Pair them with earplugs for extra defense if the noise is extreme.

Balancing Silence and Awareness

Completely blocking out sound can be disorienting. If you need to hear your boss call your name or a timer beep, absolute noise cancellation might be overkill. Some headphone models let you adjust levels or pass through certain sounds. White noise machines also allow you to stay partially connected; you'll still hear loud events, but small background chatter fades away. Deciding on the right balance depends on your environment and how crucial it is to catch certain signals.

Handling Social Interactions

If you wear noise-canceling headphones or earplugs around others, they might assume you're tuning them out or being anti-social. Letting friends or coworkers know, "I get easily overwhelmed by background sounds," can help them understand you're not ignoring them; you're managing a genuine need. Most people respect that honesty and might even admire you for taking care of yourself.

Setting Communication Signals

If you share a space with family or roommates, agree on a system. Maybe you'll wave or tap a shoulder to get attention if someone is wearing headphones. Or you'll set times when you're noise-free (like a daily quiet hour).

This fosters respect: they won't barge in shouting questions while you're in your noise-free zone, and you'll reciprocate when they need quiet. Gentle humor can help: "If I look like a hermit with these headphones on, I promise it's me, not you—I just need serenity!"

Meeting Etiquette

In offices, wearing headphones during team meetings may be frowned upon, but you can use them while prepping for a meeting or doing solo tasks. If your colleagues know you're more productive with fewer noise disruptions, they might support your choice.

For essential meetings or personal convos, you remove them, but you can mention, "After the meeting, I'll pop my headphones back on so I can wrap up this project." This signals your intention to focus without being aloof.

When to Seek Professional Advice

If noise sensitivity severely impacts your daily life, consider talking to a therapist or an occupational therapist specializing in sensory issues. They can suggest coping methods or even exercises that gradually build noise tolerance. Sometimes, underlying conditions like hyperacusis or misophonia might need specialized attention.

Hearing Tests

If you find you're extremely bothered by normal-volume sounds or you suspect hearing damage, a hearing test might clarify the situation. Hearing loss can lead to auditory distortions or heightened sensitivity to certain frequencies. An audiologist can guide you toward the right treatments or hearing protection strategies.

Workplace Accommodations

In certain jobs, you may have the right to request noise modifications. This could be a quieter workspace, permission to wear noise-canceling headphones, or scheduling tasks in a low-noise area.

If you believe your performance is suffering due to constant noise, explore whether your employer can provide accommodations under relevant laws or company policies. A conversation with HR might open doors to a more comfortable environment.

Maintaining a Noise-Managed Lifestyle

Don't feel obliged to use the same solution all day. Perhaps you use noise-canceling headphones in the morning, then swap to softer earplugs after lunch, or let a white noise app run in the evening. Rotating gear can help you avoid headphone fatigue or the discomfort of earplugs worn too long. Also, different tasks demand different levels of hearing. You might want partial awareness while cooking but near silence during deep writing.

Regular Breaks

Continuous headphone or earplug use might leave you disoriented. Schedule small breaks where you remove them and let your ears adjust. If you're in a safe, relatively quiet place, a few minutes of normal hearing can reset your senses. This also helps avoid ear irritation or sweating under headphone cups.

Clean and Maintain Devices

Headphones, earplugs, and white noise machines need basic care. Wipe earcup cushions with a gentle cloth, replace foam earplug pairs regularly (or wash reusable ones as instructed), and occasionally dust your white noise device. A little maintenance keeps them hygienic and extends their life. If your headphones use rechargeable batteries, store them properly so they don't degrade.

Stay Flexible

Your noise needs might fluctuate from day to day. Some days you can handle mild background chatter, others you need quiet because you're anxious or overstimulated. Listen to those cues. Don't force yourself to always rely on earplugs if you're in a calm environment, but don't hesitate to use them if a mild environment suddenly becomes chaotic. Adaptation is key—noise control shouldn't feel like a prison but rather a supportive tool.

Crafting Your Sound Sanctuary

Noise-reduction aids aren't about creating a mute world—just a friendlier one. By choosing the right tools, you shield yourself from the random chaos that interrupts focus or ruffles your nerves. Whether you rely on noise-canceling headphones, simple earplugs, or a cozy blanket of white noise, each method helps reclaim mental space once lost to distractions. Plus, it's a form of self-care: acknowledging that your ears and mind deserve a break from the clamor around you.

Don't feel guilty if you enjoy soft background tunes or cafe chatter. Noise management is personal—some prefer partial sound, others need near-silence. The key is awareness. Recognize when noise is a problem and act on it, rather than suffering in silence (or the lack thereof). That might mean adjusting your environment, scheduling quiet periods, or pulling out the headphones at the first sign of chaos.

With a bit of trial and error, you'll discover the sweet spot that keeps your mind calm, your work sharp, and your ears happily unburdened by the din of modern life.

20

Clear Physical Clutter

Have you ever tried to focus at your desk only to notice a random pile of papers, an old coffee mug, and a tangle of chargers invading your space? It's like having a crowd at a concert you didn't invite. For many people, especially those prone to sensory overload or with neurodivergent minds, physical clutter can spark mental clutter. Your eyes dart from object to object, your hands fidget, and suddenly you're distracted by the sheer chaos.

Clearing physical clutter isn't about becoming a minimalist monk or ditching all your worldly goods—it's about creating an environment where your brain can breathe. In this chapter, we'll look at why a tidy workspace matters, how to keep items where they belong, and simple daily routines to ensure you don't drown in stuff.

Why Clutter Can Be So Overwhelming

When your desk is strewn with files, papers, and random knickknacks, your eyes take it all in whether you want to or not. Each item competes for a slice of your attention. Imagine trying to read a book in a room where 50 different TV screens flash images simultaneously.

Over time, the constant visual stimulation wears you down. It's no wonder you may feel drained or easily distracted. By paring down what's in your direct line of sight, you reduce the number of things your brain has to process.

Tactile Distractions

Physical clutter isn't just about what you see. If your work area is cluttered, you might knock items over, shuffle piles to find a pen or keep bumping your elbow against random objects. Each of these small irritations breaks your flow. For those who are sensitive to touch or easily irritated by having to move items around, a clutter-free zone can be a haven, letting you move gracefully without snagging on stuff.

Mental Chaos Connection

There's a reason people say "clean space, clear mind." When you look around and see disorder, it can feed into the feeling that your thoughts are scattered too. On the flip side, an organized environment can have a calming effect: your mind mirrors the tidy space, making it easier to focus on tasks at hand. This doesn't mean everything must be magazine-cover perfect. It just means the clutter isn't actively shouting at you, "Deal with me! Or else!"

Emotional Weight

We sometimes hold onto objects for sentimental reasons, or out of fear we might need them "someday." Over time, these items can pile up, leaving you feeling weighed down every time you glance at them.

It might be an old sweater, a broken gadget you keep meaning to fix, or outdated papers "just in case." While it's healthy to keep meaningful items, it's also healthy to let go of what truly no longer serves you. This lightening of your physical load can also lighten your emotional load.

The Right Place for Everything

One of the simplest ways to tackle clutter is to designate zones. For example, your desk could have a small zone for stationery (pens, color-coded sticky notes), another for your computer gear, and maybe a spot for personal items (like your phone or a water bottle).

When you pick something up, you should know exactly where it lives. Apply the same principle more broadly: a shelf in the closet for seasonal items, a basket by the door for your keys and wallet, or labeled boxes for art supplies. Clear zones offer a map for your belongings, so objects don't drift into random corners.

The "One In, One Out" Rule

This trick helps prevent piles from growing again. Every time you bring something new into your space, you let go of something similar. It's a gentle way to keep the total number of items stable instead of ballooning. If you buy a new coffee mug you love, maybe you pass along one of your older mugs to a friend or donate it. This rule might feel weird at first, but it forces you to consider if you need multiples of the same item.

Containers and Labels

When your belongings have dedicated containers, clutter is more easily contained (pun fully intended). Transparent containers let you see what's inside without rummaging. If transparency isn't your style, label the box or bin clearly. This helps you find items quickly and reduces the friction of cleanup.

Instead of thinking, "Where do I toss this random cable?" you know it belongs in the labeled "Cords and Chargers" box. And if you spot a box sitting around for weeks, that's a sign you may not need what's in it. Except for the box of cables, you always need to keep those.

Storage That Fits Your Life

Everyone's storage needs differ. Some prefer open shelving, where items are visible and within reach. Others hate seeing stuff and want closed cabinets or drawers. If you're the type who forgets about objects you can't see, open shelves or clear bins might be ideal. If, however, you find open shelves visually distracting, closed cabinets or opaque boxes might suit you better. The goal is to tailor your storage approach so that it fits your brain's quirks and habits, not someone else's Instagram aesthetic.

Simple, Daily Maintenance Routines

Sometimes, clutter builds up not because we lack storage, but because we lack a habit of putting things away promptly. The "two-minute tidy" is a quick solution: once or twice a day, spend exactly two minutes returning items to their rightful homes. You'd be amazed how much can be done in 120 seconds—throw away scraps, stow pens, straighten a stack of papers. It might seem trivial, but doing it regularly prevents clutter from mushrooming overnight.

End-of-Day Reset

If you work at a desk or use a particular spot for hobbies, do a short "reset" before you call it a day. File or set aside papers, cap your pens, close open tabs on your computer if relevant, and place any stray objects where they belong. This routine only takes a few minutes, yet it means you arrive the next morning with a clean slate. That sense of freshness can boost motivation and reduce the chance of starting your day in frustration.

Weekly Deeper Sweep

While daily upkeep keeps clutter from exploding, a weekly session tackles dust bunnies or hidden messes you might miss day-to-day. This might involve wiping surfaces, emptying trash bins, sorting mail, or doing a quick inventory of what's piling up. If you find random items that don't serve a purpose, consider discarding or donating them. By scheduling this deeper sweep, you prevent clutter from nesting in overlooked spots (like the back of drawers or under furniture).

The "One Task at a Time" Approach

Cleaning can feel endless if you try to do it all at once. To avoid overwhelm, pick just one small area each day or each week to focus on—a single drawer, the corner of your desk, or one shelf. Give that area some love: remove items, wipe it down, and decide what returns. That's it. Over several weeks, you'll gradually tame the entire space, but you won't burn out by attempting a marathon cleaning spree.

Handling Sentimental Items

A big reason clutter persists is emotional attachment. Maybe it's old birthday cards, your first work badge, or a child's craft project from years ago. These items carry memories, so parting with them can feel like losing the memory itself. But realistically, you can't keep every object from your entire life. The emotional trap is when you hold onto things you never use or even look at, just because they remind you of a moment.

Taking Photos or Scanning

One tactic is to preserve the memory without keeping the physical item. Snap a photo of that old T-shirt or scan the doodle your friend made for you in high school. Store these images digitally in a folder labeled "memories." This way, you can revisit them anytime without letting boxes of old stuff swallow your closet. A glance through photos can evoke the same nostalgia, minus the physical clutter.

Setting Boundaries

It's helpful to set a limit on sentimental items: maybe one box for keepsakes, or one shelf dedicated to nostalgia. If that space is full, you must remove something before adding another. This rule pushes you to be selective, keeping only the truly precious pieces. It also ensures sentimental clutter doesn't quietly expand throughout your home.

Enlisting a Friend

If you struggle, ask a friend or family member for help. They can be a voice of reason: "Do you really need 18 stuffed animals from childhood?" They might gently challenge your attachments or reassure you that letting go of an item doesn't mean forgetting the memory. Pick someone who respects your emotions but can also help you see realistically.

The Benefits of a Clutter-Free Zone

When your environment is streamlined, your brain can latch onto the task at hand. You're not scanning the table for a pen under piles of stuff. You're not half-distracted by the leaning tower of books. You simply do what you need to do. This is especially liberating if you have ADHD or are prone to daydreaming—fewer objects screaming for your attention means fewer opportunities to derail yourself.

Reduced Stress and Anxiety

Visual order can have a calming effect. Walking into a relatively tidy room often feels like a deep exhale. Sure, some might argue that a little mess sparks creativity, but that mess should be a conscious, contained one, not a swirl of random objects. By controlling physical clutter, you send a signal to yourself that you're in control of at least this corner of your life. That sense of control can ripple into other areas, making you feel more balanced.

Easier to Clean

Dusting a cluttered space is a pain. You have to move each item, dust underneath, and then put it back in exactly the right spot—assuming you remember that spot. A clear desk or a simple shelf arrangement takes minutes to wipe down. Cleaning time shrinks dramatically when you don't have to maneuver around endless objects. Over the long run, that time saved adds up to do more of what you love.

Welcoming to Others

If you live or work with others, a de-cluttered environment is often more inviting. Friends, family, or coworkers can navigate easily without fear of toppling a precarious stack. If you host a small gathering, you won't be rushing around shoving items in closets at the last second. And if you share the space day-to-day, your neat approach can inspire others or at least set a standard.

Clearing the Clutter Mines

- **The Perfection Trap:** Aim for progress, not a show-home. You don't need color-coded files and pristine empty surfaces if that's not your style. A little clutter is okay, but it should be clutter you're comfortable with, not clutter that's controlling you.
- **"I'll Do It Later" Syndrome:** Procrastination is clutter's best friend. If you tell yourself, "I'll put this away next time," items can mount quickly. Use the daily or weekly routines mentioned earlier. Doing small tasks promptly is easier than doing big tasks later.
- **Overbuying Organizers:** Sometimes people buy fancy bins and racks, hoping the new gear will solve everything. But if you're just piling the same old junk into prettier containers, the root issue remains. Organize after you purge or at least decide what you want to keep, not before.
- **Neglecting Maintenance:** Even the best system fails if you don't maintain it. If you stash items properly for a week then revert to old habits, clutter creeps back. The daily two-minute tidy or end-of-day reset ensures your efforts don't unravel.
- **Handling Others' Stuff:** If you share a space, it's tricky. You can't just toss your partner's collection of vintage baseball caps or your

roommate's random craft supplies. Communicate boundaries and negotiate common areas. If they're not on board, consider designating separate zones so your minimal approach isn't undone by their piles.

Balancing Minimalism and Practicality

Minimalism can be freeing, but not everyone wants bare walls and three possessions. Perhaps you're a book lover who finds comfort in rows of novels, or a chef who likes having multiple gadgets. That's fine. The goal is to avoid random junk that serves no purpose or clutters your daily tasks. If an item brings genuine joy or functional value, it can have a place.

Keeping Frequently Used Items Accessible

Some mistakenly stash everything out of sight, then get annoyed having to dig out the stapler 20 times a day. The trick is balancing easy access with neatness. Keep daily essentials within reach—like your favorite pen on the desk or your phone charger near the outlet. Items you seldom use go deeper in drawers or higher on shelves, so they don't crowd your immediate workspace.

Rotating Seasonal or Specialized Gear

If you have seasonal items—like winter blankets, holiday decorations, or summer sports equipment—store them away when they're off-season. That frees daily space from objects you won't touch for months. Similarly, if you have a hobby that you do intensively for a while, then pause, and stow those supplies neatly until you're ready to pick it up again.

Making Peace with Your Space

Clearing physical clutter isn't about living in a sterile box. It's about ensuring your environment doesn't work against you. Every item you keep has a purpose or a real joy it brings, rather than just being another stray object. By

CLEAR PHYSICAL CLUTTER

finding spots for your belongings, cleaning in small bursts, and respecting your emotional attachments, you build a space that supports focus and calm instead of draining you.

As with any habit, the shift to a tidier environment won't happen overnight. Give yourself grace if you slip back into the occasional messy spree. The beauty of daily or weekly resets is that they offer a fresh start repeatedly.

Each time you tidy, you strengthen that muscle, making it easier next round. Over time, you'll likely find you feel lighter, more organized, and more at peace in your workspace—a pretty good payoff for the relatively small effort it takes to put things back where they belong.

21

Sensory-Friendly Clothing

You're rushing out the door when you realize the tag on your new shirt is scratching the back of your neck. Five minutes later, you're squirming in the car, tugging at the collar. It's not a big deal—until it is. For many inside and outside of the neurodivergent community, clothing can become a constant irritation rather than a cozy shield.

A texture here, a too-tight seam there, a scratchy fabric tag—it all adds up, becoming a low-level distraction that's hard to shake. The solution? Sensory-friendly clothing. In this chapter, we'll explore how to pick clothes that don't nag at your skin, strategies for building a comfortable wardrobe, and why these choices can help you navigate each day with a bit more ease and focus.

Clothing Comfort Matters

Ever try to focus on a project while your socks are itching or your waistband is digging in? It's like a tiny mosquito buzzing around your brain—irritating enough to break your concentration in a million small ways. If you're neurodivergent and already prone to sensory overload, even a minor clothing discomfort can tip the scales from "managing fine" to "seriously annoyed." Comfortable clothing acts like an invisible ally, letting you forget you're even wearing anything and simply get on with your day.

Stress and Sensory Overload

Clothing is in contact with your body all day, so an uncomfortable fabric can heighten your stress response over time. Imagine if your shirt collar keeps pinching at your neck—your body remains on mild alert, sapping mental energy. For those sensitive to textures, certain materials (like rough wool or cheaply made synthetics) can trigger bigger reactions, from constant itching to full-blown meltdowns if you can't escape the feeling. Opting for gentler fabrics can lower that baseline stress, giving you extra emotional bandwidth for the tasks ahead.

The Joy of Effortless Dressing

When your clothes feel good, there's a sense of ease. You slip into a soft cotton T-shirt or a pair of well-fitted jeans, and you barely register them afterward. It's like your outfit merges with you, not fighting for attention. This quiet comfort can boost confidence. Instead of spending mental energy on a scratchy sleeve, you can focus on your morning routine, your commute, or your next creative project. That small shift from "I notice my clothes all the time" to "I never think about them" can be surprisingly freeing.

Healthier Skin

Irritation from certain materials doesn't just cause mental distraction; it can also affect your skin. Repeated rubbing or sweating in non-breathable fabrics might lead to rashes or breakouts. If you're someone who struggles with eczema or frequent skin issues, choosing hypoallergenic or breathable fabrics can be a significant step in easing discomfort. Your body and mind both benefit from a kinder texture against your skin.

Challenging Materials/Sensations

Think about the worst clothing experiences you've had. Was it that wool sweater that felt like sandpaper? A pair of nylon socks that made your feet clammy? Or that fancy top with tags so big they could double as a sail? People's triggers vary, but some usual suspects include:

- **Wool or scratchy synthetics:** Rough against the skin.
- **Tight elastics or seams:** Pinching or leaving marks.
- **Large tags or thick labels:** Constant scraping.
- **Un-breathable fabrics:** Lead to sweat and discomfort.

Test Runs

Before committing to new clothing, do a mini "sensory test." If you're in a store, rub the fabric between your fingers or try the garment on if possible. Move around—bend, stretch, see if anything pokes or constricts. For online shopping, read fabric descriptions carefully. If "100% wool" has always been your enemy, you might avoid it. Some brands list "tag-free" or "flat seams," which can be a blessing for sensitive wearers.

Temperature Sensitivity

Some folks run hot, others run cold. Fabrics that make one person cozy might leave another sweating. If you overheat easily, lighter materials like cotton, bamboo, or linen could be your friends. If you're always chilly, a soft fleece or plush jacket might help. Mind the layering too—multiple thin layers can regulate temperature better than a single thick sweater, letting you adapt if the day's weather shifts or you move between heated and unheated spaces.

Seams and Stitching

Seams aren't always top-of-mind—until you feel one digging into your foot or shoulder. Check the inside of socks for thick toe seams, or shirts with large, ridged stitching. Some companies sell seamless socks or shirts specifically designed for sensory sensitivities. Or look for "flat-lock seams," which lie smoother against your body. If the seam is rough, you might be able to flip the garment inside out (especially for T-shirts) to see if it feels better worn that way at home, although maybe not for public outings.

Building a Comfort-First Wardrobe

Think about what you wear most often—underwear, socks, T-shirts. These are the foundations of your wardrobe and usually the closest to your skin. Prioritize comfortable versions of these essentials. For instance, some brands focus on soft, tag-free underwear or seamless bras that minimize pinching and rubbing. If you spend the majority of your day in these basics, upgrading them to high-comfort versions yields a big payoff.

Natural vs. Synthetic Fabrics

Natural fibers like cotton, bamboo, or linen often feel softer and let the skin breathe. They also tend to have fewer chemical treatments (though not always—some are still heavily processed). Synthetics can be comfortable, too, especially newer tech fabrics designed for sports or moisture-wicking. The key is to avoid cheap, scratchy blends. Pay attention to how the fabric is woven or finished. A quality cotton T-shirt can feel worlds apart from a budget polyester top that squeaks when you move.

Capsule Wardrobe Thinking

A "capsule wardrobe" is a small collection of versatile pieces that mix and match. If you're minimalistic or easily overwhelmed by choice, consider this approach. It means fewer items, but each is comfortable, fits well, and can be paired with everything else. For instance, you might have a few neutral pants and a handful of tops in your favorite soft fabrics. Then you're not scouring a huge closet each morning—just picking from curated, comfy staples.

Embracing What Works

If you find an incredibly comfy shirt, consider buying it in multiple colors or stocking up if your budget allows. No rule says you can't have duplicates of something that suits you perfectly. Some neurodivergent individuals love wearing nearly the same outfit style daily because it removes decision fatigue and ensures consistent comfort. If variety isn't important to you, feel free to keep it simple. If you crave variety, focus on different colors or subtle style changes, but stick to the same trusted fabric types.

Strategies to Maintain Comfort

Don't suffer a scratchy tag. Many clothes let you cut out the tag, though be careful not to slice the fabric. If a label is stubbornly stitched in, consider a seam ripper or tailor's help. If certain seams are tight, a tailor might be able to adjust them. Small alterations, like adding a soft lining to a waistband, can transform an otherwise irritating garment. Think of these adjustments as minor surgeries that greatly extend the life and wearability of your clothes.

Pre-Washing New Clothes

New garments sometimes have stiff sizing or leftover chemicals from manufacturing. A quick wash often softens them. If you're especially sensitive, consider adding an extra rinse cycle or using fragrance-free, gentle detergents. This step can also help you gauge if the garment will remain comfy after it shrinks a bit or loses that initial stiffness.

Rotate Shoes and Accessories

Comfort isn't limited to shirts and pants—shoes and accessories matter too. Shoes that pinch or rub can ruin your day. Rotate pairs so you're not always wearing the same style that stresses one part of your foot. If belts, watches, or jewelry irritate your skin, explore alternative materials (fabric belts, silicone watch straps) or more relaxed styles (stretchy belts, clip bracelets). You don't have to ditch these items entirely—just find versions that don't sabotage your comfort.

Plan for Varying Weather

If you live in a place with changing seasons, stash away out-of-season clothes so they're not cluttering your closet. Then, when the temperature shifts, you bring out the cozy sweaters or the breezy shorts. Also, layering can be your best friend. A soft tank top under a sweater can shield you from a scratchy wool interior, or a lightweight jacket can help you adapt if the temperature changes midday. This way, you're always prepared without wearing an uncomfortable piece all day.

Social and Professional Settings

Some workplaces or events have dress codes—formal business attire, uniforms, etc. If you're required to wear something that rubs you the wrong way, see if you can tweak it. For instance, wearing a cotton undershirt under a stiff blazer might help. If the standard uniform is collared and tight, maybe your manager will let you get a larger size or a softer variant if you explain your sensory needs. In many places, a polite conversation about needing minor accommodations can open doors you didn't know were there.

Subtle Adaptations

If everyone around you wears certain types of clothing that you find irritating, you can incorporate small adjustments. For instance, if formal shoes kill your feet, try orthotic insoles or padded socks. If formal shirts scratch, pick one made of the same color and cut but in a softer blend. Often, people won't even notice these changes, but your comfort level skyrockets.

Addressing Reactions

Sometimes friends or colleagues might tease you about always wearing the "same style of shirt" or wonder why you cut out tags. You can keep your explanations brief—"I'm more comfortable without tags," or "I have sensitivity to certain fabrics." Most people will respect that, especially if you mention it helps you focus or feel less stressed. It's your body—why not dress it in a way that feels good?

Handling Kids' Clothing

If you have children, they may display strong preferences or meltdowns about certain clothes. Encourage them to articulate what feels wrong—"It's too tight," "The label hurts," "It's scratchy." Help them discover what textures they do like—maybe soft cotton or fleecy pajamas. This fosters self-awareness about their needs. Buying kid-friendly, tag-free lines or letting them pick from a limited set of comfy options can reduce morning battles.

Preparing for Sensory Surprises

Kids often grow quickly. Last month's comfy socks might suddenly be too snug. Keep an eye on signs of discomfort—fidgeting, complaining, or reluctance to wear something. Regularly check if they need new sizes or if a garment that used to be fine now triggers them. Forcing a child to endure scratchy clothes often backfires; better to find something they'll keep on without fuss.

Don't Forget the Socks

- **Ignoring Seasonal Swaps:** Wearing your thick wool sweater in spring can lead to sweaty frustration. Periodically swap out seasonal clothes so you're not rummaging through items that don't suit the weather.
- **Impulse Buys Without Testing:** That sale might look tempting, but if you don't check the fabric or fit, it might end up a closet dweller. Whenever possible, do a quick comfort test or read reviews about how the fabric feels.
- **Clinging to Worn-Out Favorites:** We all have that beloved T-shirt from a decade ago, full of holes. If it no longer fits or the fabric is pilled and scratchy, consider replacing it with a similar but fresher version. Nostalgia is nice, but you deserve actual comfort.
- **Overlooking Under-layers:** Sometimes you can salvage an itchy sweater by wearing a soft undershirt or slip. If you forget this option, you might banish a garment unnecessarily. Try layering solutions before you toss something entirely.
- **Forgetting Laundry Effects:** Harsh detergents or hot drying cycles can make fabrics stiffer or shrink them oddly. If your clothes start feeling rough, change your laundry routine—use gentle detergent, cooler water, or hang-dry certain items to maintain softness.

Comfort as a Productivity Booster

When your clothes aren't nagging you every five minutes, you can devote those mental microseconds to work, hobbies, or simply enjoying life. This added focus can boost productivity in subtle ways—like finishing a task 10 minutes quicker or avoiding a meltdown that costs you an hour of regrouping. Multiply that over weeks, and it's a real gain.

Boosted Mood and Confidence

Feeling comfortable in your skin translates to feeling comfortable in your clothes. When you're not fussing over a bra strap or a scratchy seam, you stand taller—literally and metaphorically. That comfort radiates outward. People often sense you're at ease, which can make social or work interactions smoother. Confidence isn't always about wearing the fanciest outfit; sometimes it's just about wearing something that lets you forget your clothes altogether.

Self-Care Mindset

Choosing sensory-friendly clothing can be a form of self-care. It's a tangible way of saying, "I deserve to feel good, not stressed, in my daily life." Even if the rest of your day gets chaotic, your shirt won't be adding to your stress pile. That small act of kindness to yourself can set a tone of mindfulness and well-being throughout your routines.

Fewer Spikes in Sensory Overload

If you're prone to feeling overwhelmed by multiple stimuli, comfortable clothing removes one potential trigger. That means if a loud noise or a strong smell occurs, you still have the mental capacity left to handle it. Instead of layering discomfort—scratchy clothes plus noise plus bright lights—you only deal with two triggers instead of three. The fewer annoyances, the better your odds of maintaining calm.

Crafting Your Clothing Comfort Plan

- **Audit Your Closet:** Spend an afternoon checking each item. Does it feel good? If not, can it be altered or layered for comfort? If not, maybe it's time to donate or toss it.
- **Focus on Essentials:** Invest in high-quality, soft basics like underwear,

socks, and daily T-shirts. These are the pillars of comfort.
- **Try Before You Buy:** If possible, shop in-store to feel fabrics. If online, check return policies or read fabric details carefully.
- **Plan Wardrobe Updates:** Slowly replace old, irritating clothes with more sensory-friendly versions. No need for a massive overhaul overnight—small steps keep it budget-friendly.
- **Keep Reassessing:** As seasons change or your body changes, re-check the comfort of your wardrobe. Stay open to evolving needs.

Dressing Without Stress

Wearing comfy clothes can seriously boost your mood and help you get stuff done. Choose soft fabrics, ditch those annoying tags, and pick outfits that you don't have to keep fiddling with. This way, you can focus on your work and let your creativity flow without any distractions.

Remember, comfort is king! Don't force yourself to wear clothes that look good but feel awful. Your clothes have a big impact on how you feel, how much you get done, and your overall well-being.

22

Intentional Lighting

Sitting at your desk, your eyes squint under a harsh fluorescent glare. Across the room, someone has opened the curtains, and a beam of morning sunlight slices right into your face. You try to keep working, but it's like your brain keeps skipping a beat every time that brightness hits.

For humans, neurodivergent or not, lighting can significantly influence mood, focus, and comfort. Yet we often just flip a switch and let whatever overhead bulb is there define our day. This chapter explores how to adjust brightness and color temperature to your liking, plus practical tips for picking the right lamps, bulbs, and ways to harness or filter natural sunlight. Because when you have lighting that matches your mind's rhythm, life becomes a little easier on the eyes.

Lighting Matters

Lighting isn't just about seeing your keyboard. It can shape your entire emotional landscape. Think of a soft, warm glow that turns a room cozy in the evening. Now contrast that with bright, flickering fluorescents that make you feel like you're in a hospital corridor.

Light influences how awake or relaxed we feel, how we perceive color, and how our brains process the environment. For neurodivergent individuals, certain lights can be overstimulating—leading to headaches or anxiety—

while gentle, more customized lighting can soothe the senses, paving the way for calmer thinking or better focus.

Biological Cues

Our bodies have an internal clock—often called the circadian rhythm—that relies in part on light cues. Sunlight in the morning helps signal "wake up, world!" to our brains, while dimmer light in the evening nudges us toward rest. If you're surrounded by bright, bluish light late at night, your brain might think it's still daytime, messing up your sleep schedule. By choosing the right color temperature and brightness levels at different times, you align your environment better with your body's natural cycles, leading to better sleep and smoother days.

Visual Comfort vs. Visual Stress

If the lighting is too dim, you might strain your eyes. Too bright, and you might squint or develop tension headaches. For some, flickering lights (like old-school fluorescents) can cause a sense of disorientation or even migraines. Striking the balance between not-too-bright and not-too-dim is key—especially if you're reading, working on a computer, or engaging in fine-detail tasks. Intentional lighting means being mindful of these factors, instead of living with whatever random bulb happens to be in the lamp.

Brightness and Color Temperature

Gone are the days when we judged bulbs solely by watts—modern LED bulbs might use 10 watts but shine like an old 60-watt incandescent. Lumens measure brightness. The higher the lumens, the brighter the light. For a small desk lamp, maybe 400–600 lumens is enough. For a full room, you might want multiple bulbs adding up to 2,000 or more lumens. But personal preference matters: some folks prefer a more subdued glow, while others like a robust beam so they never strain.

Color Temperature

Color temperature is measured in Kelvin (K). Lower Kelvins (around 2,700–3,000K) give a warm, yellowish glow—think of a cozy living room lamp. Around 4,000K is a neutral or "cool white," often found in offices. Moving into 5,000–6,500K, you get a bluish daylight tone—like midday sun. Warmer light (lower Kelvin) can feel relaxing but might make you sleepy if you need to be alert. Cooler light (higher Kelvin) can boost concentration but might feel harsh or clinical. Sometimes, using warm light in the evening and cooler, brighter light in the daytime helps mimic natural daylight cycles.

Flicker and CRI

Some lights flicker imperceptibly. While many people don't notice, it can be a deal-breaker for those sensitive to movement or migraines. LEDs of high quality often flicker less, but cheap ones might still cause issues. The Color Rendering Index (CRI) measures how accurately colors appear under the light—100 is the best (like natural daylight). A CRI of 80 or above is generally recommended if you want colors to look normal. For tasks like painting, photography, or design, a higher CRI can make a real difference in seeing accurate hues.

Crafting a Light-Friendly Environment

Relying on a single overhead fixture can be jarring, creating stark shadows or a too-intense glare. Instead, think in layers: ambient (general room light), task (focused light for reading or working), and accent (small lamps for mood or highlighting a particular corner). Each layer can have its own brightness and color temperature. So if you're reading at night, you might switch off the overhead and use a warm, soft lamp by your chair. For work, you might keep the overhead on but add a bright, cool desk lamp that spotlights your task area.

Positioning Lamps

Lamps at eye level can reduce overhead glare. If a bulb beams directly into your eyes, it might cause discomfort. Angle your desk lamp so it illuminates your workspace but isn't shining right at your face or your monitor. If the sun is streaming in from a window, consider adjusting blinds or curtains to diffuse harsh rays. For those who like natural sunlight but find it too bright, a thin curtain or a window film can let light in without the full glare. Position your furniture so you're not constantly squinting against a window or a lamp.

Smart Bulbs and Dimmers

If you crave maximum control, consider installing dimmer switches or using smart bulbs. With a dimmer, you can adjust brightness to your mood or task. Maybe you crank it up in the morning to wake up, then dial it down in the afternoon for a calmer vibe. Smart bulbs can even change color temperature throughout the day automatically—warm in the evening, cool midday. Some let you pick from infinite shades, though be careful not to get lost playing with your phone app for hours. The main perk is flexibility: no more fiddling with lamp changes to achieve just the right glow.

Avoiding Screen Glare

If you work on a computer, glare is often an enemy. Position your screen so it's not reflecting a lamp or window behind you. You might add a small desk lamp aimed at the keyboard but angled away from the screen. Or use a monitor hood or an anti-glare screen protector. The goal is to avoid big bright spots that fight the clarity of what's on your monitor. Subtle adjustments can dramatically reduce eye fatigue.

Harnessing Natural Light

Sunlight can boost mood, regulate circadian rhythms, and help you feel more connected to the outside world. If you have windows, letting in daylight during the morning can help you wake up gently. For those working from home, setting your desk near a window can provide a dynamic light that changes through the day, offering a sense of time's passage that artificial lights can't match. But be aware of direct glare if the sun comes straight into your eyes or onto your screen.

Using Curtains or Blinds Wisely

Not all sunlight is gentle—sometimes it's harsh, washing out your room or heating it like a greenhouse. Sheer curtains can filter light, softening its intensity without plunging you into darkness. Venetian or vertical blinds let you tilt slats to direct rays away from your face. If you get intense afternoon sun, you might close the blinds partially during peak hours, then reopen them as the sun angle shifts. This interplay keeps the environment comfortable instead of scorching.

Seasonal Affective Disorder (SAD)

Some people struggle with low mood in winter when daylight is scarce. Full-spectrum or daylight lamps can help supplement. These are designed to mimic natural sunlight, often in the 5,000–6,500K range, with a high CRI. Sitting near such a lamp for short periods can help regulate circadian rhythms and improve mood. Even if you don't have a formal SAD diagnosis, bright, daylight-like bulbs in winter months might help you feel more alert when mornings and evenings are dark.

Lighting for Neurodivergent Needs

If overhead lights flicker or hum (even if you don't notice it), it can be maddening. Some workplaces still use old fluorescent tubes that cause that imperceptible flicker. If you find it's draining your mental energy or triggering headaches, see if you can switch them off and use desk lamps or request a swap to LED panels. If you can't control the overhead lighting, wearing a brimmed cap or tinted glasses might mitigate some flicker or brightness.

Calming Corners

For individuals prone to sensory overload, having a "low-stimulation" corner with soft, warm lights can be a refuge. Maybe it's a corner of your living room or a separate room entirely. You keep the bulbs dim, possibly color them with a warmer hue, and remove overhead sources. Add cozy cushions, a warm lamp, or LED fairy lights. This space serves as a mental reset area: whenever you feel overwhelmed, you retreat there to decompress in gentler lighting.

Task-Specific Adjustments

Different tasks require different lighting. Writing or detailed work might need brighter, cooler light to keep you engaged. Meditation or reading for pleasure might need a softer, warmer tone. If you're easily distracted by shadows or reflections, a simple ring light or well-placed lamp can create an even illumination. For those with ADHD, sometimes adding a small color-changing lamp can provide a gentle focal point while you concentrate—just ensure it doesn't become a bigger distraction.

Maintenance and Ongoing Tweaks

Don't wait for bulbs to burn out to change your lighting environment. If you discover a certain lamp's too harsh, replace the bulb with a lower lumen or warmer temperature bulb. Keep spares on hand if you find a perfect type—manufacturers change models, and you don't want to lose that sweet, just-right glow if your only bulb breaks.

Cleaning Fixtures

Dust on lampshades or bulbs can dim light or create odd shadows. A quick wipe or gentle vacuum of lampshades can restore clarity. Glass covers or reflectors might get cloudy over time—removing them carefully and wiping them with a soft cloth can boost brightness. While it's minor upkeep, it ensures your lighting remains consistent.

Periodic Self-Check

Our lighting preferences evolve. Maybe you used to love a bright, daylight lamp but now find it too intense. Or your new routine means you work more at dusk, requiring different levels of brightness. Every few months, take stock: do you feel the lighting still supports your needs, or is it too sharp, too dull, or too cool in color? Make small adjustments. Even shifting a lamp a few inches might solve a mild glare problem.

Seasonal Updates

As seasons shift, you might crave different lighting. In summer, letting in more natural light can help you feel in sync with the sunny weather, but you might also want heavier curtains to block the scorching midday sun. In winter, add a lamp or two to fight the gloom. Being flexible ensures you're not stuck with a year-round configuration that only works for one season's daylight patterns.

Common Lighting Issues

- **Glare on Screens:** Adjust your monitor angle or reposition your lamp. Consider anti-glare screen protectors. If a window's behind you, reposition so you're not in the direct path of sunlight bouncing on the screen.
- **Bulbs Too Harsh:** If your eyes hurt, pick a lower lumen count or a warmer color temperature. Adding a lampshade or using frosted bulbs can diffuse the light. Dimmer switches, if possible, are an easy fix.
- **Dim Lighting That Strains Eyes:** Increase the bulb lumens or add a task lamp. If you're reading, direct the lamp so it illuminates the page from behind your shoulder—reducing shadows on your book.
- **Flickering or Buzzing:** Replace old fluorescent tubes or cheap LED bulbs with higher-quality, flicker-free versions. If wiring issues cause flickering, consult an electrician. A subtle flicker can sabotage comfort.
- **Rooms Without Windows:** Supplement with a daylight simulator lamp, especially if you spend hours in a windowless workspace. A "happy light" at your desk can mimic natural brightness, lifting mood and energy.

Striking the Balance

While lighting can significantly impact well-being, it's easy to fall into a rabbit hole, constantly adjusting brightness or color temperature. Give yourself time to settle into a setup before tweaking it again. The goal is a supportive environment, not daily lamp rearranging.

Incorporate Personal Style

Lighting doesn't have to be purely functional. If you love the aesthetic of fairy lights, neon signs, or vintage lamps, blend them in. Just ensure they don't conflict with your comfort. Maybe you plug in fairy lights for ambiance but keep them on a separate switch for times you want a more subdued or professional vibe.

Collaborate in Shared Spaces

If you share a home or workspace, talk to others about lighting preferences. Some may prefer bright overhead lights, others might want subdued lamps. A compromise might be to keep overhead lights off or dim while offering personal desk lamps for those who want more brightness. Communication fosters harmony—nobody wants a lighting war.

Keep Adapting

As your daily routine or sensitivities evolve, so may your lighting needs. Children grow, seasons change, and job tasks shift. Stay open to adjusting. Maybe you move to a new desk or discover a new lamp that fits your style. The beauty of lighting is that small changes—replacing a bulb or shifting a lamp—can have a huge impact on comfort.

A Partner, Not an Afterthought

Intentional lighting transforms a room from just "lit" to truly supportive, bridging the gap between harsh overhead glare and cozy, functional brilliance. We often take light for granted until we realize how much it shapes our day—whether it's a sunbeam that warms our morning or a soft lamp that eases us to sleep. For neurodivergent individuals or anyone sensitive to the environment, the right lighting can reduce stress, sharpen focus, and protect emotional well-being.

Think of lighting as a partner in your daily life, working alongside you, not against you. With a few thoughtful changes—picking bulbs with a suitable color temperature, layering your light sources, and harnessing natural sunlight effectively—you can set the tone for better productivity and a calmer mind. And if you discover that the best solution is a quirky combination of fairy lights, a warm desk lamp, and half-opened blinds, more power to you.

The real point is feeling at ease, so you can focus on what you love rather than waging a constant battle against the glare or dimness around you.

23

Movement While Working

You're in the middle of a project when your legs start twitching. Maybe you tap your foot on the floor, shift in your seat, or try to stretch one leg out under the desk. Eventually, you realize you've been hunched over for two hours, and your body's practically begging for a break.

For those who crave movement, sitting still can feel like a form of torture. The good news is you don't have to choose between being productive and staying active. From standing desks to gentle exercises you can do right at your workstation, you can weave movement into your work routine without losing focus. We talked about small, short breaks with movement earlier in the book. In this chapter, we'll explore ways to keep your body engaged for longer periods while your mind tackles those tasks.

Why Movement Matters for the Mind

Contrary to what some office cultures suggest, being glued to a chair isn't the key to deep concentration. Our brains often work better when our bodies aren't locked in one position. Movement boosts blood flow, delivering oxygen to your brain and releasing chemicals that support attention.

Mild physical activity can reduce restlessness and channel excess energy more constructively. That's why pacing around can sometimes help you think through a problem, or a quick stretch can jolt you out of mental fog.

Movement and mental clarity go hand in hand.

Fighting the Sedentary Blues

Sitting for extended periods can lead to stiffness, poor posture, or just a nagging sense that your body's asleep. Over time, excessive sedentary behavior contributes to health risks like obesity, heart issues, and muscle weakness. Incorporating bursts of movement throughout your workday counteracts those risks.

Even small shifts—standing for ten minutes, pedaling a desk bike at a leisurely pace—help keep your circulation going. This fosters a sense of well-being that can translate into sharper focus and more consistent energy levels.

Stress and Mood Benefits

Ever notice how a brief walk outside or a short stretch break can lighten your mood? Movement can act like a pressure valve, releasing tension. If you're juggling multiple tasks or battling anxiety, gentle physical activity can ground you, offering a mental reset.

For many neurodivergent individuals, allowing for fidgeting or light exercise while working helps manage restlessness, smoothing out those spikes of stress. Even a minute of shifting positions can keep you from hitting that mid-afternoon slump.

Balancing Energy Fluctuations

Some folks experience ups and downs in energy during the day. Movement-based work setups—like standing desks or active sitting—help harness these fluctuations more effectively. When you feel your energy dip, a brief spell of standing or pedaling can nudge you back into alertness.

On days when you're already buzzing with extra energy, you can channel that into pedal strokes or gentle swaying at a standing desk, avoiding that "caged animal" feeling that static desk setups might cause.

Standing Desks

Standing desks became a trend in recent years, with pictures of hip start-up offices featuring employees perched at tall stations, mug in hand. The idea is that humans weren't built to sit all day.

By standing part of the time, you engage core muscles, shift your weight, and naturally move more. This can reduce lower back strain compared to prolonged sitting—though it's not a magic cure, as standing too long can also be tough on your feet and legs.

Adjustability Is Key

If you're eyeing a standing desk, look for an adjustable one. You'll want to switch between sitting and standing throughout the day. A motorized desk lets you push a button to raise or lower the surface, while a manual one might require some effort to adjust.

Being able to tweak the height is crucial so you're not hunching your shoulders or tilting your wrists awkwardly. You want the desk surface at about elbow height, with your monitor roughly at eye level. This reduces strain on your neck and helps keep posture natural.

Helpful Accessories

Standing on a hard floor for hours can quickly wear out your feet, so consider an anti-fatigue mat. This cushioned surface relieves pressure on your joints and encourages subtle shifts of your feet.

Some people also keep a small stool under their standing desk to rest one foot at a time. For those who love fidgeting, you might try a wobble board or balance board, letting you sway gently. Just make sure it doesn't distract you more than it helps.

Transitioning Gradually

If you've been sitting 40 hours a week for years, jumping to a full-time standing setup might be jarring. Start with short intervals—stand for 15–20 minutes each hour, then sit the rest. Increase that time as you get used to it.

Pay attention to how your feet and back feel. If you're sore, it may be you're standing too long or that your desk height or posture needs adjustment. Over time, you'll find a standing-sitting ratio that suits your body.

To Pedal or Not to Pedal

Desk bikes or under-desk pedal units let you move your legs as you type, read, or join video calls. It's like having a mini stationary bike under your table. The motion can help restless legs, burn a few extra calories, and keep your circulation going.

If you're someone who fidgets constantly, pedaling can offer a structured outlet for that energy. Rather than jiggling your foot on the floor, you're channeling that momentum into a mild workout.

Distraction vs. Focus

One concern: will focusing on pedaling distract you from the task? Surprisingly, many find the opposite. The repetitive, low-intensity motion can anchor wandering thoughts—similar to how some people doodle while listening to a lecture. That said, if you're pedaling hard or leaning side to side, it may break your focus.

The key is gentle movement. Keep resistance moderate, so you're not gasping for air. The idea is to keep your legs moving without hijacking your attention.

Practical Setups

An under-desk pedal is often smaller and cheaper than a full desk bike (which is a stationary bike with a tabletop attached). Make sure the unit fits under your desk without your knees hitting the underside. Check adjustable resistance settings, so you can fine-tune it.

If your desk space is limited, measure carefully or consider a foldable pedal option you can stow away. Some companies offer "bike desks" in communal office areas, though this might be more for break times unless you're comfortable pedaling while coworkers pass by.

Health Boost

While you won't replicate a full gym session, pedaling for even 30 minutes a day can improve circulation and maintain leg strength. It's especially beneficial if you have long periods of sitting. Over a week, these short sessions can add up. You might pedal lightly while on calls or when sorting emails—moments that don't require intense mental calculations. Just be sure the motion doesn't cause your camera to shake if you're on a video call. A stable floor or a good mat can help.

Gentle Movement to Stay Focused

If you can't invest in a standing desk or desk bike, there are simpler ways to incorporate movement. Every 30–60 minutes do a 1-minute stretch: roll your shoulders, extend your arms overhead, wiggle your fingers, or stand up for a quick quad stretch.

These micro-breaks offer instant relief, preventing stiffness and giving your brain a tiny reset. You don't even have to leave your desk; just push your chair back slightly and use the space around you to move.

Chair Yoga

Chair yoga poses let you stretch and strengthen without leaving your seat. You might do a seated twist, gently turning to look over your shoulder, or lift one knee at a time to stretch your lower back. If your ankles or wrists get tense, circular rotations can help. These low-key moves reduce tension and keep your body from locking up. Just ensure your chair is stable—no rolling across the office mid-pose.

Standing or Walking Phone Calls

If your job involves phone calls, try standing or pacing a bit while you talk (assuming you're using a headset or speakerphone). That changes your posture and engages your muscles more than staying seated. For longer calls, you can walk around the room or even do light chores like tidying your desk if it doesn't distract from the conversation. Over time, these small steps accumulate into a healthier daily total of movement.

Fidget Tools

Some neurodivergent people find that gentle fidgeting—like rolling a stress ball under their foot or squeezing a hand grip—keeps restlessness at bay. If large movements (like pacing) are impractical in your setting, fidgets provide an outlet for that kinetic energy. A foot roller under the desk, a small pedal, or even a standing wobble-board for short intervals can be enough. The trick is picking a tool that aids concentration, not one that becomes a toy you can't put down.

Addressing Concerns and Myths

Contrary to the fear that movement ruins focus, moderate activity can sharpen it. The brain often likes gentle, repetitive motion—it's why people doodle or pace when thinking. As long as you're not sprinting on a treadmill, the movement can be a backdrop that keeps your hands or legs engaged while your mind zeroes in on the task. Experiment with small steps first, like standing for ten minutes or using a slow pedal, and see how it feels.

"I Don't Have Space"

You might worry there's no room for a standing desk or a desk bike. In smaller offices or home setups, measure carefully. Some standing desks are compact or designed to fit in corners. Desk bikes often have smaller footprints than you'd think—some models slide partly under a traditional desk. For extremely tight spots, consider collapsible under-desk pedals that you can tuck away when not in use.

"It's Disruptive to Coworkers"

If you work in an open-plan office, a desk bike might draw stares (or curiosity). However many workplaces are increasingly open to flexible setups that promote well-being. Check with HR or your manager—there may even be a wellness program that supports alternative desks.

If your pedaling is quiet and you're not bouncing around, it's often not a big deal. Alternatively, position your workstation so your gentle movements won't rattle neighboring desks. Or you can just use it during times with fewer colleagues around, like early morning or late afternoon.

"Only for the Super Fit"

Movement while working isn't about triathlon training; it's about mild motion that keeps you from going stiff. Standing for a few minutes or pedaling lightly doesn't require athletic prowess. Even if you're out of shape or dealing with physical limitations, small shifts in posture or slow pedal strokes can be beneficial. The focus is on comfort and energy management, not completing the Tour de France from your desk.

Integrating Movement Routines into Your Day

Begin with achievable goals. Maybe try a "stand for 15 minutes every hour" approach, or pedal lightly during your morning email check. If you like it, extend the time. This incremental method helps your body adapt, preventing aches from sudden overuse. Also, check your posture—switching from a seated slump to standing at a desk can highlight new tension if you're not aligned properly.

Schedule Movement Blocks

If your job requires intense focus for stretches, schedule short intervals to move afterward. For instance, after 45 minutes of deep work, stand and do a mini stretch. Or pedal for 5–10 minutes, then sit again. Putting these blocks in your calendar or using a reminder on your phone ensures you don't forget. These micro sessions refresh your body and mind, so you return to the task more alert.

Alternate Tools

You don't have to stick to just a standing desk or just a bike. Some people keep both: standing for a while, then sitting with a pedal. Or, if your budget is limited, a stool that allows you to sit semi-upright can provide a moderate posture shift. Over time, you'll figure out which combination best suits your tasks. Maybe you enjoy standing for phone calls but prefer pedaling when reading documents.

Listen to Your Body

If your legs ache or your feet get sore, don't push through blindly. Adjust. Raise or lower your desk, tweak your seat height, or reduce the resistance on your bike pedals. The point is to find a gentle, sustainable level of movement, not to punish your body. Pay attention to any persistent discomfort—your body might be telling you that the desk or bike setup is off, or that you need more breaks.

Moving Through The Day

- **Overdoing It:** Feeling enthusiastic, you might stand for hours straight or pedal at high resistance. This can lead to muscle fatigue or joint pain. Build up gradually. Listen to any discomfort.
- **Ignoring Posture:** Standing incorrectly or hunching over while pedaling can still strain your back or neck. Keep your workspace ergonomics in check—monitor at eye level, arms relaxed, shoulders down.
- **Neglecting Regular Breaks:** Movement while working is great, but you still need breaks from the mental aspect. Stepping away from your workstation for fresh air or a quick walk is vital for overall well-being.
- **Over-Distraction:** If you find yourself focusing more on pedaling stats than the spreadsheet you're supposed to finish, dial back. The movement should be the background, not the main event.
- **Expecting Instant Miracles:** Changing your workspace to allow movement is beneficial, but it won't solve all issues overnight. Give your body time to adapt. Movement is one piece of the puzzle—sleep, diet, and stress management still matter.

Moving Your Way Through the Day

Movement at work doesn't have to be complicated or flashy. It can be as simple as standing up to stretch, pacing during a phone call, or pedaling under your desk while you draft emails. These small motions break up the monotony of static sitting, letting your body stay engaged and your mind stay sharper. Over time, you might find you're less achy, more alert, and better able to handle the day's tasks.

Yes, you might get a few curious looks if you're the first in your office to adopt a standing desk or a desk bike. But as more folks learn the benefits of blending activity into their work, you could become the trendsetter who helped everyone else get out of their chairs. And if a standing desk or fancy bike isn't feasible, don't fret—those micro-break stretches and gentle chair exercises can still do wonders.

The ultimate goal is to let your body be part of your work process, not a passive passenger along for the ride. Give your legs, back, and restless spirit a chance to move, and watch how it subtly transforms your workday.

24

Use Labeled Storage

Try recalling the last time you needed a specific item—maybe a stapler or a certain charging cable—and you ransacked multiple drawers and boxes before finding it. Or worse, never found it at all. For many, this moment is painfully familiar.

Labeled storage can be the difference between a smooth day and a chaotic quest. By giving every folder, box, or shelf a clear name, you make it infinitely easier to store and retrieve things without upending your whole space. In this chapter, we'll explore the magic of labeled storage, share tips for keeping your labeling system simple, and highlight some pitfalls to dodge along the way.

Why Labeling Is So Essential

When you see a box boldly marked "Pens" or a folder labeled "Receipts," your brain barely has to think. You know exactly what goes inside. That "no-brainer" aspect saves mental energy and time—no more rummaging through unknown boxes or flipping open multiple folders. Especially for those who can get overwhelmed by too many choices, a label provides a quick anchor point. It's like a neon sign shouting, "Put it here!" or "Find it here!" So if your desk is scattered with random items, a system of labeled containers can channel those items into their rightful spot with minimal cognitive overhead.

Reducing Clutter Anxiety

When items have designated, labeled homes, clutter often doesn't pile up in random nooks. If something is out of place, it's obvious. A sheet of paper belongs in "Bills—Paid" or "Bills—Unpaid," not floating around. This structure also alleviates the stress of "Where does this go?" because the system answers that for you. Over time, that clarity can keep your environment tidier, your tasks more trackable, and your mind calmer.

Quick Recovery from Chaos

Even if your space momentarily explodes in a flurry of activity—like prepping for a project or sorting incoming mail—a labeled system can help you bounce back fast. Let's say you had to haul out boxes of craft supplies for a weekend project. Afterward, you're not guessing "Which box had the glue sticks?" You read the labels: "Craft Supplies—Glue & Tape," done. Within minutes, everything's back where it belongs. Think of labeling as a roadmap: you might detour into messy territory, but it's straightforward to get back on track.

Keeping Others in Sync

If you live or work with others, unlabeled storage can lead to baffling "Where did you put my stuff?" exchanges. With labels, your roommate, partner, or coworkers can store or retrieve items without asking you repeatedly. This fosters shared ownership of the space. Everyone who sees "Office Supplies—Markers" or "Pantry—Snacks" knows exactly what's inside. No more chaotic rummaging or accidental mix-ups, like storing nails in the box meant for holiday decorations.

Basic Principles of Labeled Storage

Labeling doesn't have to mean elaborate color-coded tags or a complicated naming convention. In fact, the simpler, the better. A piece of tape and a Sharpie often suffice. If you do prefer a label maker or fancy stickers, that's great—just don't get so wrapped up in a design that you procrastinate labeling. The prime goal is clarity: it should be readable at a glance.

One Category per Container

Avoid the danger of turning one box into a multi-category stash. If you label a single bin "Office Supplies & Random Stuff," you've lost the clarity. Instead, separate "Office Supplies—Staples, Tape" from "Miscellaneous Tech Cables." This way, each container holds a single category or subcategory. You can nest categories ("Office Supplies—Pens" and "Office Supplies—Paperclips") if you have multiple small containers within a larger box. But each container still gets its label.

Labels on Both Ends or in Easy View

If you'll store a box on a shelf, consider putting a label on the front and the top (or at least on the side you can see). That way, whether you're scanning from above or rummaging face-on, you spot the label. If you store boxes in a closet, place labels outward so you don't have to slide each box out to read the top. The aim is to see the label with minimal effort—no twisting or turning required.

Consistent Wording

If you label one folder "Taxes 2023," don't label the next one "Bills from 2022." Keep a consistent format, like "Taxes—2023," "Taxes—2022," "Bills—2023," "Bills—2022." This uniformity, whether by year or topic, helps your brain know where to look. Mixed naming, like "Old Bills" vs.

"Invoices 2022," can confuse you or others later. If you have subcategories (e.g., "Bills—Paid," "Bills—Unpaid"), maintain that pattern across the board.

Low-effort, High-value Labeling

If you enjoy visuals, assign colors to broad categories. Maybe green means finances, blue means personal projects, and red means urgent tasks. Then, on the label, you not only write the name but also use a small colored dot or tape. This is optional but can help you spot categories quickly. Just be sure to keep a mental or posted "key" if you use many colors.

Using Icons or Pictures

For kids' rooms or if you prefer a quick visual cue, print or draw small icons. Example: a pencil icon for "School Supplies," a shirt icon for "Clothes—Winter," etc. This approach also helps non-readers or those who process images faster than text. Just keep the icons consistent (e.g., the same pencil image for all office supply boxes) so you don't accidentally mix them up.

QR Code Method

For the tech-savvy, you could label boxes with a QR code that links to a digital inventory (like a Google Sheet listing the contents). This is overkill for everyday items but can be handy for infrequently accessed boxes—like holiday decorations or archived documents. When you scan the code, you see exactly what's inside without opening the box. Just remember to update the inventory if you add or remove items.

Labeled Drawer Dividers

Drawers often become chaos central—pens, sticky notes, and random junk all jumbled. Drawer dividers with small labels can corral the madness. "Pens," "Markers," "Sticky Notes," and "Tape," each having its little compartment. If you change your mind later (e.g., you no longer keep markers), peel off or rewrite the label. This micro-organization in drawers saves rummaging time daily.

Don't Get Lost in Labels

While labeling is great, labeling every single item can be pointless. "Pencil" on a pencil might be silly, though it's comedic. Keep labels for containers or categories, not each tiny item. Too many labels can become visual noise. Strike a balance—label boxes, shelves, and folders, but skip labeling each pen or binder clip.

Over-complicated Categories

If your labels sound like a law firm's filing system ("Insurance Documents for Q1 2023, Subsection Home & Auto, Subsection Pending"), you might struggle to maintain or remember them. Streamline. "Insurance—2023," "Insurance—2022," etc. Keep it direct and minimal so you're not decoding a cryptic code each time you open a box.

Inconsistent Updates

A label is useless if the contents change and the label doesn't. If you empty a box of "Electronics—Chargers" and refill it with "Holiday Decorations," but keep the old label, you'll sow confusion down the road. Make it a quick habit: if you re-purpose a container, replace the label immediately. Otherwise, you'll revert to rummaging frustration.

Label Illegibility

Handwritten scrawls can be fine if you read your writing easily. But if your scribble looks like hieroglyphics, you might need a label maker or at least a clear penmanship approach. Labels should be legible from a comfortable viewing distance—no squinting or guessing. If you do like fancy fonts or design flair, ensure they remain readable.

Fear of Renaming

Sometimes we label a box "Winter Clothes" but end up using it for spring jackets, too. Don't hesitate to rename or refine as your needs evolve. A label isn't a locked contract—feel free to peel it off or place a new one on top. It's your system, not a museum exhibit. Being flexible keeps your labeling relevant.

Simple and Sustainable Systems

When you pick something up to store, aim to place it in the correct labeled spot right away. This "one touch" philosophy prevents piles of items waiting for a second wave of organization. For instance, if you finish with a batch of receipts—immediately drop them in "Receipts—To File," not on a random corner of your desk. The next time you handle them might be final filing, but at least they're corralled in the right zone.

Routines for Maintenance

Just like we discussed in earlier chapters about daily or weekly tidying, labeling thrives on upkeep. Once a week, do a quick scan. Are items sitting on surfaces that belong in labeled boxes? Did you rummage through something and forget to put it back properly? That 5–10 minutes of re-labeling or re-storing ensures your system doesn't degrade into chaos. Think of it as a mini alignment check.

Periodic Audits

Every few months, glance over your labeled containers. Any that have become dumping grounds for random junk again? Perhaps you can create a new category or realize you no longer need that container. Maybe "Old Projects" can now be merged with "Archived Work" or tossed if it's obsolete. Regularly auditing keeps your labels from drifting into inaccuracy. It's like giving your system a tune-up.

Make it Social

If you share space, ensure everyone understands the labeling logic. Show them how you've categorized things—like "Craft Supplies—Paint," "Kitchen—Spices," or "Office—Incoming Mail." Encourage them to follow the same pattern. A collaborative approach helps them feel ownership, making it more likely they'll put items back correctly instead of random stash.

The Labeled System

When everything is systematically labeled, retrieving or storing an item is a breeze. You save minutes daily—minutes that add up over months or years. This is particularly beneficial in workplaces where multiple people handle shared supplies or in a busy household with a rotating cast of family members rummaging for stuff. Efficiency soared because you know exactly where each item belongs.

Less Stress, More Mental Space

As we've discussed, messy piles often create low-grade stress, even if you don't consciously dwell on them. A labeled environment fosters calm. You see "Office—Paperclips," and there are the paperclips, not jumbled with pens and random receipts. No mental friction, no frustration. That sense of calm can extend to your overall mindset because you're not living in a mild panic about losing or misplacing things.

Encourages De-cluttering

Labels indirectly encourage you to keep categories from ballooning. If you have a box labeled "Misc Tech Cables" and it's overflowing, you might realize it's time to weed out those old phone chargers from 2005. The label acts like a boundary, gently reminding you: "Here's what you decided was for cables—if it doesn't fit, maybe it's time to part ways."

Future-Proofs Your Organization

Even as your life evolves—new hobbies, new job, new location—having a labeling mindset helps you adapt. Need a new box for knitting supplies? Slap a label on it and you're good. The fundamental approach remains the same, so your system can expand or contract without losing coherence. Over time, you become a pro at swiftly reorganizing after big changes.

Label for Ease

Using labeled storage isn't about micromanaging your life into tiny compartments. It's about clarity and ease, ensuring each item has a place that's signposted for you (and anyone else who shares your space). You don't need to label every knickknack, but picking prime categories significantly cuts down on the daily rummage dance.

Yes, you might slip up—tossing an item into the wrong box in a hurry. Or you might realize a label no longer suits the container's contents because you changed your mind about its purpose. That's okay. Systems evolve, and labels can be peeled off or rewritten.

As long as you keep it straightforward and maintain it, labeling can bring a refreshing sense of order to your daily routines. You'll recover precious minutes you used to spend searching, and you'll find an unexpected calm whenever you open a shelf or closet. No more rummaging, no more guesswork—just a few seconds to read a label and put or grab exactly what you need.

Your Mind, Your Way

We've traveled through a wide landscape of ideas—quick hacks, mindset boosters, and sensory-friendly solutions—to help you harness your strengths and tackle challenges in a way that feels right for your unique mind.

But how do you wrap up a project like this, one that brims with a variety of methods, tools, and philosophies? It isn't about memorizing every single chapter or feeling pressured to put all the strategies into practice at once. The real goal is to notice what resonates.

Maybe your big takeaway was discovering micro-tasks to end procrastination, or perhaps you found a new love for color-coded notes. You might have realized that certain bright lights give you headaches, and you're now eyeing an adjustable lamp. Or maybe you feel less alone in your experiences after reading stories about neurodivergent minds forging their paths. Whatever you gleaned, the important step is weaving it into your daily life in small, consistent ways.

Productivity Is Personal

Some folks thrive in a bustling coffee shop, typed lines dancing across the screen as they sip lattes. Others need quiet corners, free from flickering lights and tapping feet. One person might doodle and color-code everything, while another needs a minimal digital workspace with zero notifications. There's no single, universal solution. That's the heart of why so many ideas appeared in these chapters. The perfect system isn't the one that scores top reviews online—it's the one that flows with how **your** mind naturally operates.

It can be tempting to compare yourself to someone else who seems to have it all figured out: that coworker who flawlessly manages a jam-packed schedule, or the friend who always picks the perfect time to work out, meal prep, and read a novel before bed. But you're not them.

You carry your mental patterns, emotional triggers, and energy cycles. When you craft a routine or pick a new tool, do it with the intent of honoring your rhythms. If your best ideas bloom around midnight, there's no shame in that. If you simply **can't** face certain tasks until you've had a midday break, schedule those tasks in the afternoon.

By tailoring these hacks to you, you'll find a sustainable path rather than a forced routine that crumbles after a week or two.

Experiment, Adapt, Refine

You might be the type who loves diving into new methods, setting them up in intricate detail. Or maybe you test ideas slowly—one small change at a time. Regardless, it's important to see each strategy as an experiment.

If something doesn't click, that's okay. You can tweak it, blend it with another concept, or set it aside for now. No hack is sacred. They're all just potential tools waiting for your stamp. Take time to acknowledge your progress along the way. Small wins, like completing a single task or refining a routine, build momentum toward bigger breakthroughs.

Let's say you try micro-tasking. Maybe you break a project into smaller parts but still feel overwhelmed. Ask why. Are your chunks still too big? Did you try to tackle them at low-energy times? Perhaps you simply need a bit more structure—like tying each micro-task to a timed block or scheduling them after you've warmed up with a simpler job. By iterating instead of discarding the method entirely, you keep refining it until it fits.

Adaptation also matters when your life changes. A trick that worked last year may feel clunky if you start a new job or experience a shift in family duties. Your schedule might morph from flexible blocks to school drop-offs and pick-ups. That's normal. Return to these pages and see if there's a fresh spin on an older method, or craft a brand-new approach that suits your updated reality.

Keeping a Light Touch

You might have noticed a consistent theme in the chapters: be kind to yourself. Whether it's facing clutter or forging routines, guilt can sneak in—maybe you tried to color-code tasks and ended up with a rainbow meltdown on your desk. That's just part of the process.

If something fails or if you skip a day, show yourself patience. The point of a productivity approach isn't to fill your day with hyper-efficiency or track every second. The real aim is to build a supportive framework that respects your mental health, your attention needs, and your day-to-day complexities.

This also applies to how you read (or re-read) the material. Feel free to skim chapters, skip around, or re-visit a particular section that fits your current struggle. The layout is meant to let you drop in for a quick tip or a 10-minute refresher.

If you don't need a certain strategy—like body doubling or a standing desk—there's no rule that you must adopt it. Maybe you're happier with your existing environment. Perhaps you only needed fresh ideas on balancing a flexible schedule. Take what's useful, leave what isn't, and trust your instincts on which tools fit your style.

Growing Your Toolkit

Just as you reached the last chapters, you might have felt you're only at the start of understanding how your mind works best. That's a great place to be—curious, open, and ready to refine your methods. Below are a few pointers for continuing your self-education and staying linked with communities who share these interests:

- **Try a New Resource or Author:** Check out other productivity authors or talk with friends who have tried their own hacks. Books like *Atomic Habits* by James Clear or *Getting Things Done* by David Allen might offer additional angles. No single book can cover every possible scenario, so keep an eye out for voices that spark something in you.

- **Explore Online Communities:** Look for groups (like the one I've created called "The ND Mind") that center on neurodivergent experiences. These spaces let you ask questions, share breakthroughs, and even find accountability buddies. Many communities exist on social platforms or in dedicated forums. Engaging with people on a similar journey reduces isolation and opens new perspectives. You might discover that someone else solved a problem you're grappling with, or you might provide the tip they've been needing.
- **Consider Coaching or Mentorship:** If you feel stuck, a productivity coach or therapist familiar with neurodivergent minds can help tailor strategies to your life. They can spot blind spots or offer subtle tweaks you hadn't considered. Sometimes, an outside perspective is key to unlocking your next level of productivity or emotional well-being.
- **Local Meetups or Workshops:** Some cities have meetups for time management, bullet journaling, co-working, or ADHD support groups. Joining one can feed you fresh ideas, let you test new approaches in a supportive setting, and help you see that you're far from alone. Even a single workshop could jump-start your routine changes.
- **Self-Reflection Tools:** Keep a short journal or log of what you try—like a mini "productivity diary." Jot down which hacks you tested, how they felt, and whether they improved your day. Over a month, you'll build a record of successes and flops, making it easier to weed out what doesn't serve you. This reflection habit can become a go-to resource whenever you face new challenges.
- **Think About Larger Goals:** Productivity isn't just about checking items off a list. Step back and ask: "What bigger vision do I have for my life?" Maybe it's building a creative career, being an attentive parent, or traveling more. Each hack or routine is just a stepping stone toward that broader aim. Keeping your larger "why" in view can motivate you to keep experimenting and refining.

Coaching, Forums, and "The ND Mind"

Many times, we assume we can fix everything alone, but it's completely fine—and often smart—to reach out for guidance. Coaches who specialize in neurodivergent traits can tailor your approach, pointing out patterns you might not see. Forums or local groups can provide a sense of belonging.

Meanwhile, "The ND Mind," if you're interested, offers an online hub for people exploring these concepts. It's a place to chat about ADHD, autism, dyslexia, or other neurological setups, all while swapping tips on staying productive or just surviving the daily swirl of tasks. If you ever feel alone in your struggles, stepping into these supportive spaces can remind you that there's an entire community walking a similar path.

Strength and Self-Discovery

People sometimes ask: "If I'm neurodivergent or if I have trouble focusing, do I need to fix myself?" The answer is: absolutely not. This isn't about erasing who you are. It's about unveiling the ways your mind can flourish once it's matched with the right environment and the right strategies. Productivity, at its heart, is about progress, not perfection. It's about growth, adaptability, and honoring your unique approach to life's challenges.

You're not broken. Society's norms about how tasks "should" be done often ignore the diversity of thought processes out there. By reading this book, you've already taken a step to break out of that one-size-fits-all mold. You're claiming your own blueprint.

As you step back into your life—jobs, family, passions, random errands—carry a fresh awareness of how your mind operates. Notice the times you get locked in hyper-focus or realize you've taken on too many tasks at once. Remember that you have tools: a color-coded list, a mindful transition method, or that cunningly placed timer on your desk. You're not just reacting anymore; you're shaping your day in a way that respects who you are.

Keep testing your boundaries, from discovering new types of noise-canceling headphones to reorganizing your closet with labeled boxes. Keep noticing how your environment influences your concentration, from the glare of fluorescent lights to the thickness of a sweater seam. Stay open to the chance that a hack that flopped at first might work wonders next year, or you might turn a casual approach into your new normal.

Forward Motion

Productivity isn't a fixed destination—there's no final test awarding you the gold star of success. Instead, it's an ongoing conversation between your mind, your environment, and your goals.

If you ever find yourself in doubt—maybe because you had a tough week or an unexpected life event shook your routine—return to these pages or connect with others who embrace their difference. Often, you'll rediscover that your mind isn't the problem, just the methods that don't fit it.

Above all, be gentle with yourself. Keep an eye on each bright spot in your progress, each small victory that once seemed impossible. It doesn't matter if it's clearing a single desk drawer, finishing a chapter of a book, or surviving a noisy café by using headphones. Each milestone deserves applause—some might even deserve a little celebration or a quick text to a friend saying, "Hey, guess what I just did!"

You now hold a toolkit of hacks and concepts. Feel free to keep adding to it, editing it, and even ditching what no longer serves you. Because at the core, productivity isn't about squeezing the most hours from your day or turning yourself into a task robot. It's about guiding your life in a direction that resonates with your values and talents, minus the guilt and overwhelm. It's about being the person you want to be—in the quiet hours of the morning or the midnight hush—while still finishing what needs to be done.

May these final words remind you that your brain is your ally, not your adversary. The tips in these chapters will guide you, but your intuition, curiosity, and willingness to adapt are what transform them into real change. It's your story. So, experiment boldly, pivot gracefully, lean on the community around you, and let each day bring a little more self-discovery. In time, you'll gather a stable of personal strategies—some brand new, some borrowed—that keep you on a path of progress and peace.

Here's to staying true to your mind's quirks and strengths. Here's to trusting the small steps that lead to big victories. And here's to realizing that productivity isn't about doing it all—it's about doing what matters in a way that honors who you are.

About the Author

Eric is a father, business owner, and productivity enthusiast with a passion for helping others navigate life in ways that honor their unique strengths. As a neurodivergent individual and parent to neurodivergent kids, Eric understands firsthand the joys and challenges that come with thinking differently.

Drawing from personal experiences, professional expertise, and years of trial and error, Eric has developed a deep appreciation for practical tools, adaptive strategies, and the power of community. Whether it's coaching others, building supportive spaces like "The ND Mind," or simply swapping stories, Eric is committed to fostering understanding and growth for neurodivergent minds and those who love them.

When not working, writing, or connecting with others, Eric cherishes time with those close to him and finds peace and inspiration exploring nature through hikes and kayaking adventures. He lives in the metro Atlanta area with his kids, embracing the vibrant chaos of everyday life.

This book is a reflection of Eric's belief in progress, not perfection, and a heartfelt invitation for readers to discover tools and approaches that truly work for them so they can acknowledge their progress.

Subscribe to my newsletter:
✉ https://theneurodivergentmind.substack.com

www.ingramcontent.com/pod-product-compliance
Lightning Source LLC
Chambersburg PA
CBHW062048080426
42734CB00012B/2581